Thea is a specialist planning and environmental law practitioner at No5 Chambers and is consistently rated as one of the leading juniors at the planning and environmental bar. Thea was included in the Planner's Women of Influence list for 2021.

Thea has a diverse practice specialising in the promotion of development with particular expertise in solar energy, and major residential development. Thea is an experienced inquiry advocate and regularly advises on project design and amendment, strategy, and prospects of success.

Thea is listed in the Legal 500 and Chambers and Partners which notes that she is *"Really good with clients, really good on her feet and exceptional with detail. Her work ethic is brilliant." "Incredibly thorough, incredibly focused and also a very engaging person. A great advocate."* Thea is ranked in Band 1 for Planning.

A Practical Guide to the Law and Policy of Solar Energy Development

A Practical Guide to the Law and Policy of Solar Energy Development

Thea Osmund-Smith LLB
Barrister, No5 Chambers

Law Brief Publishing

Published 2022 by Law Brief Publishing, an imprint of Law Brief Publishing Ltd
30 The Parks
Minehead
Somerset
TA24 8BT

www.lawbriefpublishing.com

Paperback: 978-1-914608-30-8

To Mam for your advice and wisdom,
Dad for your generous encouragement,
Lee and Airleia for your patience and support,
and Nova for your grounding indifference.

Thanks also to Gail Stoten for championing me
and setting me off on this path,
and for teaching me so much.

PREFACE

Solar energy development is about to be very big. The support for large scale solar energy development at a national level and in emerging government policy is unequivocal – a position that has led to a significant increase in the number of very large-scale projects in the planning system in recent times. Solar energy development is inextricably linked to the climate change agenda and the imperative to reduce greenhouse gas emissions. The UK has challenging targets to achieve its legal obligations set out in the Climate Change Act 2008, and a fundamental part of that is securing clean energy from renewable and low carbon sources. Solar energy is a well-developed and cost-effective technology that is capable of making a real contribution to meeting those targets, and to providing energy security in the UK, but it is not without controversy. Big schemes can have significant impacts, and it is up to the planning system to strike the balance between competing interests.

This book is intended to provide a short and practical guide to the law and policy relevant to solar energy development, the different routes to achieving planning consent, and issues that can arise in respect of this type of project, from scheme design to post consent. It is intended to be an introduction to solar energy development for planning practitioners across all disciplines, and it may also be of use to other stakeholders in the process such as councillors and local interest groups.

The law is believed to be correct at the time of writing; 1 July 2022.

Thea Osmund-Smith
July 2022

CONTENTS

CHAPTER ONE

BACKGROUND AND CONTEXT

Introduction

Climate Change, and its potentially catastrophic human, environmental, and societal impacts for generations young and old, is considered by many to be the greatest threat faced by humanity. The consequences of rising temperatures and extreme weather events are all too obvious, and they are being felt now; rising sea levels, increasing coastal erosion and flooding, wildfires destroying communities and valuable wildlife habitats, changing and unpredictable weather patterns and warming which threatens food production and biodiversity.

To help tackle the climate crisis, Parliament has committed to reaching net zero carbon emissions by 2050 – something which could properly be described as an enormous challenge. Rapid growth in renewable energy has a "*key role*" to play and will eventually "*underpin*" the entire net zero economy.[1] Indeed it is Government policy that the UK will need to be entirely powered by clean energy by 2035.[2]

Residential, commercial, community and utility[3] scale solar capacity in the UK currently stands at 14 gigawatts ("GW"). The costs of solar

---

1 HM Government, 'Net Zero Strategy: Build Back Greener' October 2021 available at https://www.gov.uk/government/publications/net-zero-strategy, page 19

2 Net Zero Strategy, October 2021

3 There is no single accepted definition of "utility-scale solar". It generally applies to larger schemes, or solar "farms" that generate power to feed into the grid, and I use it here in contradistinction to residential solar on the rooftops of dwellings, and commercial solar which are panels primarily

energy development have been decreasing over the past decade, and the technology and panel efficiency is consistently improving. Solar, together with wind, is now one of the cheapest forms of energy in the world.[4] The Government through its British Energy Security Strategy ("the BESS") expects solar capacity to increase five-fold by 2035 and will consult in due course on amendments to strengthen policy in favour of solar development on "non-protected" land[5] while ensuring that communities continue to play a role in the process, and that environmental protections remain in place. The strategy also notes that electricity demand is highly likely to double by 2050, which is an inevitable consequence of electrification in our daily lives.

The support for solar energy development at a national level is unequivocal:

i) December 2020's Energy White Paper[6] sets out that achieving net zero rests on a "*decisive shift*" away from fossil fuels to clean energy and describes solar as a "*key building block*" of the future energy generation mix.[7]

ii) The National Planning Policy Framework July 2021[8] ("NPPF") sets out a presumption in favour of renewables at

---

associated with a commercial business. A community project is neither solely residential, nor business scale, and may even be big enough to be regarded as "utility-scale", but they are typically smaller.

4 https://www.gov.uk/government/news/biggest-ever-renewable-energy-support-scheme-backed-by-additional-265-million

5 Not defined in the Strategy but assumed to be land not subject to any planning, landscape, ecological or other designation.

6 HM Government, Energy White Paper, 'Powering our Net Zero Future', December 2020

7 Ibid., Ministerial foreword, and page 45

8 Which can be accessed at https://www.gov.uk/government/publications/national-planning-policy-framework--2

paragraph 158, and at paragraph 152 states that the planning system should support the transition to a low carbon future in a changing climate, inter alia by supporting renewable and low carbon energy and associated infrastructure.

iii) September 2021's Draft National Policy Statement EN-1[9] states that wind and solar are the lowest cost ways of generating energy and that a secure, reliable, net zero system in 2050 is likely to be composed "*predominantly*" of wind and solar.[10]

iv) Draft National Policy Statement EN-3[11], also dated September 2021, describes solar as "*a key part*" of the government's strategy for low-cost decarbonisation of the energy sector and renewables as an "*essential*" element of the transition to net zero.[12]

v) The Net Zero Strategy establishes that the UK will be powered entirely by clean energy by 2035 (infrastructure for which needs to be deployed at an "*unprecedented scale*"), with the Government forecasting a 40-60% increase in demand over the same period.[13]

Thus, a number of overarching themes begin to emerge in the ever-evolving energy policy and guidance:

---

9 Department for Business, Energy & Industrial Strategy, 'Draft Overarching National Policy Statement for Energy (EN-1),' September 2021

10 *Ibid* at paragraph 3.3.21 G

11 Department for Business, Energy & Industrial Strategy, 'Draft National Policy Statement for Renewable Energy Infrastructure (EN-3),' September 2021

12 *Ibid* at paragraphs 1.1.1 and 2.47.1

13 HM Government, 'Net Zero Strategy: Build Back Greener' at pages 98 and 102

i) the increasing imperative to reduce greenhouse gas emissions evident in legislation (through amendments in the Climate Change Act 2008).

ii) the key role for renewable energy in meeting this challenge.

iii) the evident need to pick up the pace of decarbonisation.

iv) the fact that demand for energy will continue to increase to 2050.

v) the unprecedented scale and pace of the transition that is required; and

vi) the Government's commitment to the securing the infrastructure necessary to deliver change.

Climate change and the need for renewable energy

Renewable energy, its development, and the need for it is inextricably linked to the climate crisis but harnessing the power of renewable natural resources is not new. Waterwheels, the first hydropower installations, were in use over 2000 years ago harnessing the energy of moving water and converting it into mechanical output. Windmills became a feature of the landscape from around the 8th century, but of course, wind was exploited long before that to power sailing ships across the oceans of the world. With the advance of modern technology, there was perhaps less need to rely on sporadic and unpredictable natural resources, and by 1882, the first coal-fired power station in England, known as the Holborn Viaduct power station, began generating electricity for public consumption. The power station was the brainchild of Thomas Edison who opened a further power station later in the same year in New York which was the first commercial power station in the United States.

Fast forward just over 100 hundred years to 1985, and there was a growing awareness of the damaging impact of human activity on the planet, and the potential impact of environmental damage on human health. The Vienna Convention for the Protection of the Ozone Layer was created as a response to the growing knowledge and recognition that damage to the ozone layer "potentially"[14] posed a threat to human health. The Convention followed on from work carried out in the 1970s to better understand the cause and effect of changes in the Ozone layer and precautionary measures were already being implemented at the national and international level.

Building upon the Vienna Convention, the Montreal Protocol on Substances that Deplete the Ozone Layer followed in 1987 and was adopted on 15 September of that year. To date, it is the only UN treaty ever that has achieved the universal ratification of all 197 countries, and so can properly be termed "a global agreement." The purpose of the Protocol was to protect the ozone layer by phasing out the production and consumption of ozone-depleting substances in recognition of what was then considered the "likely"[15] adverse effects to human health that were likely to result from a damaged ozone layer.

In 1992, the United Nations adopted the United Nations Framework Convention on Climate Change ("UNFCCC") which entered into force on 21 March 1994 and has near universal membership. The UNFCCC recognised that climate change is a common concern of humankind, and that human activities had been contributing substantially to concentrations of greenhouse gases that would result in global warming. The aim of the UNFCCC is the "*stabilization of greenhouse gas concentrations in the atmosphere at a level that would prevent dangerous anthropogenic interference with the climate system. Such a level should be achieved within a time frame sufficient to allow ecosystems to adapt naturally to climate change, to ensure that food production is not threatened and to enable economic development to proceed in a sustainable manner.*[16]"

---

[14] The word used in the preamble to the Convention

[15] The word used in the preamble to the Protocol

[16] United Nations Framework Convention on Climate Change, Article 2

The UNFCCC places a greater obligation on developed countries to "take the lead in combating climate change"[17], and lays down the principles that parties should:

(i) Protect the climate for system for the benefit of present and future generations of humankind.[18]

(ii) Take precautionary measures to anticipate, prevent or minimise the causes of climate change, and not postpone such measures because of a lack of full scientific certainty.[19]

(iii) Promote sustainable development, cooperate in promoting and supporting an open international economic system that would lead to sustainable economic growth.[20]

The Commitments of the Parties are set out in Article 4 and include gathering and publishing information of the Conferences of Parties, or "COP", the most recent of which took place in 2022 in Glasgow in the United Kingdom – "COP26." Article 4 sets out a wide range of commitments to encourage positive environmental policies and measures to prevent climate change, to prepare for adaption to the impacts of climate change, and to promote the sharing of relevant information concerning climate change and response strategies.

Next came the Kyoto Protocol (1997) which entered into force on 15 February 2005 and is based on the principles of the UNFCCC committing industrialized nations to transition to limit and reduce greenhouse gas emissions in accordance with agreed individual targets. The Protocol did not apply to countries that were still considered to be developing, and so China was not required to reduce its emissions despite being among one of the major contributors of greenhouse gas emissions.

---

[17] Article 2(1)

[18] Article 3(1)

[19] Article 3(3)

[20] Article 3(4) and 3(5)

Furthermore, despite signing, the US (as the second largest contributor to greenhouse gas emissions) did not ratify the Protocol.

It is widely accepted that rising levels of carbon dioxide and other greenhouse gases are to blame for climate change, and that the increase in greenhouse gases is almost entirely due to human activity. The power sector accounts for a significant amount of global greenhouse gas emissions at around 25%, but other causes are manufacturing, and agriculture and deforestation. Of the carbon dioxide gases produced, around 43% goes into the atmosphere.[21]

The UK met its emission target for the first commitment period of 2008-2012 under the protocol, achieving a 23% reduction below base year emissions. The second commitment period covers the years 2013-2020 in which the Member States of the European Union committed to reduce emissions by 20% compared to 1990 levels; the UK has also over-achieved against that target. The 2022 UK Greenhouse Gas Emission, Final Figures statistical release published by the Department for Business, Energy & Industrial Strategy ("BEIS") on 1 February 2022[22] explains that the UK remains committed to its shared target with the EU as part of the Withdrawal Agreement[23]

A significant element of that achievement has been as a result of a two-thirds reduction in the power sector.[24] As of 2021, low carbon electricity represents over 50% of the UKs total generation,[25]. In terms of solar

---

21 https://www.gov.uk/guidance/climate-change-explained

https://assets.publishing.service.gov.uk/government/uploads/system/uploads/attachment_data/file/1051408/2020-final-greenhouse-gas-emissions-statistical-release.pdf

23 Agreement on the withdrawal of the United Kingdom of Great Britain and Northern Ireland from the European Union and the European Atomic Energy Community, Article 96

24 https://www.gov.uk/government/news/uk-enshrines-new-target-in-law-to-slash-emissions-by-78-by-2035

25 Ibid.

energy specifically, between 2010 and the end of 2021, the UK had increased capacity from 95 megawatts to approximately 14GW, and in 2021 solar photovoltaics[26] ("PV") contributed more than 10 per cent of renewable generation, and more than 4 per cent of total electricity generation in the UK.[27]

The Kyoto Protocol was effectively superseded by the Paris Agreement that was adopted by 196 Parties at COP21 in Paris on 12 December 2015, and entered into force in 2016. The Agreement required all nations, developing and developed, to commit to reducing greenhouse gas emissions and submit a plan to the UN setting out how they intended to do so. The Agreement is focused on limiting global warming to well below 2 degrees Celsius compared to pre-industrial levels, and "*pursuing efforts to limit the temperature increase to 1.5°C… recognising that this would significantly reduce the risk and impacts of climate change.*"[28]

Following the 21st Conference of the parties to the Convention, on 12 December 2015 the text of the Paris Agreement on climate change was agreed and adopted. The Paris Agreement sets out certain obligations to reduce emissions of greenhouse gases, in particular CO2, with the object of seeking to reduce the rate of increase in global warming and to contain such increase to well below 2°C above, and if possible, to 1.5°C, above pre-industrial levels. On 22 April 2016 the United Kingdom signed the Paris Agreement and on 17 November 2016 the United Kingdom ratified the Agreement. By that time, in domestic law, the Climate Change Act 2008 ("CCA 2008") had already set the ambitious target to reduce UK emissions by at least 80% by 2050 compared to 1990 levels.

---

26 The conversion of light into electricity using semi-conducting materials.

27 Department for Business, Energy & Industrial Strategy (William Spry). 'Review of solar PV Capacity Publications,' 31 March 2022, https://assets.publishing.service.gov.uk/government/uploads/system/uploads/attachment_data/file/1064817/Review_of_solar_PV_capacity_publications.pdf

28 Paris Agreement, Article 2

The Agreement requires countries to submit their plans for climate action known as "nationally determined contributions" ("NDC") by 2020. NDC are at the heart of the Paris Agreement, and the UK communicated its NDC to the UN on 12 December 2020 committing to reduce economy-wide greenhouse gas emissions by at least 68% (compared to 1990 levels) by 2030. The next NDC is required to be submitted by 2025.

At the domestic level, the CCA 2008 sets out a legally binding framework for the UK to reduce greenhouse gas emissions which was originally 80% by 2050 relative to 1990 levels. The UK was the first country to set a legally binding target, and on 27 June 2019, this target was amended, committing the UK to a legally-binding target of net zero emissions by 2050, set on a whole-economy basis.[29]

The CCA 2008 also introduced:

(i) carbon budgets, which place a restriction on the total amount of greenhouse gases that the UK can emit over a 5-year period. The first five carbon budgets covered the period from 2008-32. The UK's sixth carbon budget (2033-37) incorporated the UK's share of international aviation and shipping emissions for the first time and set a binding target to reduce emissions by 78% by 2035.[30]

(ii) the Climate Change Committee, which is an independent statutory body that advises the UK Government and Devolved Administrations on climate change mitigation and adaptation, including emissions reduction targets.

In October 2021, the Net Zero Strategy was presented to Parliament. In his foreword, the Prime Minister set out that "*[R]emoving dirty fossil fuels from the global economy will lead to the creation of vast new global industries*

[29] Incorporating international aviation emissions for the first time.

[30] The Carbon Budget Order 2021

from offshore wind to electric vehicles and carbon capture and storage."[31] The Strategy, which points to the stark consequences already being felt from climate change in the UK makes clear that renewable energy generation has a key role to play in achieving net zero emissions by 2050, and that it will "underpin" the net zero economy. The additional benefits of clean power are set out, including reduced costs, and protection from energy price spikes that are experienced in the volatile international fossil fuel markets. The ambition is to fully decarbonise the power system by 2035[32] and part of that, inevitably, is to increase the amount of renewable energy which will most likely be composed predominantly of wind and solar generation.[33]

Most recently in April 2022, the Government published the BESS noting recent events that have contributed to rising energy costs, namely the Covid-19 pandemic, and Russia's invasion of Ukraine. The BESS recognises that the UK needs a long-term flow of energy that is clean, affordable, and secure. Part of the answer to that is for British Energy to be generated in Britain using what the Prime Minister referred as "Britain's inexhaustible resources of wind and – yes – sunshine"[34]

The BESS expects a five-fold increase in the deployment of solar power by 2035,[35] and indicates that the government will in due course consult on amendments to policy to strengthen the policy support for solar development. The document expresses support for large scale projects to be located on previously developed land, or lower value land where that is possible, and notes the benefit of co-locating solar development with other functions such as agriculture, onshore wind generation, or storage.

---

[31] HM Government, 'Net Zero Strategy: Build Back Greener', October 2021 available at https://www.gov.uk/government/publications/net-zero-strategy

[32] Ibid., p.19

[33] Ibid., p.98

[34] BESS 2022, p.3

[35] BESS, p.19

The UK government acknowledges that significant increases in all forms of renewable energy capacity is required to meet with net zero targets.

Why solar[36] and why now?

Solar technology is not novel or new. Planning and environmental practitioners will have been aware of all scales of solar projects for many years and will have observed PV panels on rooftops and over fields across the country. However, the number of projects, and particularly utility scale projects that are currently in the planning system, gaining consent at a local level, and at appeal, has increased significantly over the past few years and is set to continue. That prompts the question, why?

There are a number of reasons, the most significant of which includes the positive and increasingly robust policy context and support for renewable energy development catalysed by the climate change crisis and successive binding targets flowing from that global context that now requires the UK to achieve net zero by 2050. At set out above, the cost of solar installations has also been decreasing over the past decade and solar energy now represents one of the, if not the cheapest form of renewable energy development. The Government's Contracts for Difference scheme[37] has also incentivised investment in renewable energy by ensuring that developers of expensive scheme with high upfront costs are protected from market volatility in future. Successful developers who win a contract though the auction process will be paid a fixed (indexed) rate

---

36 References to solar energy development throughout this text are to solar photovoltaic ("PV") systems unless otherwise mentioned. Solar PV development utilises specially designed panels to turn direct sunlight into energy. There are other less common types of solar energy development such as concentrated solar power, albeit the author is not aware of any such schemes in the UK. At a residential or commercial scale, solar systems might also be used which can utilise thermal panels to produce warm water and air.

37 https://www.gov.uk/government/publications/contracts-for-difference/contract-for-difference

for the electricity produced over a 15-year period, meaning that the developer can predict its future revenue. Together those factors have encouraged greater developer confidence and stimulated investment in the market.

The emphasis on a low carbon future, and the fundamental role that clean energy has to play in that will ensure the continuing importance of solar energy development in the UK's energy mix for many more years. Recent events have also affirmed the need for energy security in the UK, and the benefit of 'home-grown' renewable energy that doesn't rely on foreign and unpredictable supply. However, it should also be noted that the proliferation of solar energy development, especially where it is proposed to be located in the countryside will undoubtedly raise objection from local communities and other interested parties such as the Council for the Protection of Rural England ("CPRE"). Such objection can lead to unfortunate political intervention, even in the context of much needed renewable energy development. In 2013, the increasing levels of objection to onshore wind development prompted the intervention of Eric Pickles, the then Minister for Housing, Communities and Local Government to issue a Written Ministerial Statement ("WMS") expressing the view that planning decisions on onshore wind were not always reflecting a locally-led planning system, and that "*[M]eeting our energy goals should not be used to justify the wrong development in the wrong location.*"[38]

The WMS led to an unashamedly politically driven policy that set onshore wind scheme apart from other renewable technologies, and prevented consent from being granted unless development was in an area identified as suitable for wind energy development in the development plan; and, following consultation, it can be demonstrated that the planning impacts identified by the affected local community have been

[38] Written Ministerial Statement by Eric Pickles on local planning and onshore wind, MHCLG 6 June 2013

fully addressed and the proposal has their backing.[39] The approach has had a fundamentally negative impact on the promotion of onshore wind, with new development ceasing almost overnight. Since then, there has been a renewed emphasis on offshore wind, since unsurprisingly, people in boats, planes and helicopters appear less inclined to complain about turbines in the view. A similar intervention in respect of solar energy would be catastrophic for the industry, although floating solar projects are now being tested and delivered offshore.

[39] The policy approach remains in the current National Planning Policy Framework (2021), at footnote 54. The vast majority of Development Plans do not identify areas that are suitable for wind energy development.

CHAPTER TWO

SECURING CONSENT FOR SOLAR DEVELOPMENT – AN OVERVIEW

Introduction

There are essentially three ways to achieve consent for solar development which is dictated by the size of the project. Small scale residential and commercial projects might well fall within the scope of permitted development rights set out in the Town and Country Planning (General Permitted Development) (England) Order 2015 ("GPDO"). The GPDO grants planning permission for the classes of permitted development set out in Schedule 2. Where a landowner or occupier is entitled to rely upon such rights, there is no need to make an application for a grant of planning permission to the local planning authority ("LPA") under s.62 of the Town and Country Planning Act 1990 ("TCPA 1990").

Permitted development rights

Part 14 of Schedule 2 of the GPDO concerns renewable energy, and Class A permits the installation or alteration of solar equipment on a dwellinghouse or a block of flats, or a building situated within the curtilage[40] of a dwellinghouse or a black of flats. Paragraph A.1 further defines the right by setting out what development is excluded from Class A, such as solar PV panels that would protrude by more than 0.2 metres

[40] For discussion on curtilage, see *R. (on the application of Hampshire CC) v Blackbushe Airport Ltd* [2021] EWCA Civ 398 per Andrews LJ at [56] – [117]

beyond the plane of the wall or the roof slope upon which they are mounted. Paragraph A.2 sets out the conditions subject to which the permitted development right is granted and includes the requirement that panels (or solar thermal requirement) should, so far as practicable, be sited so as to minimise the effect on the external appearance of the building, the amenity of the area, and should be removed when they are no longer needed.

Class B of the same part permits the installation, alteration or replacement of stand-alone[41] solar equipment for microgeneration within the curtilage of a dwellinghouse or a block of flats. As with Class A, the right granted by Class B has to be read alongside Paragraphs B.1 and B.2 which define the parameters of the permitted development right. For example, development is not permitted pursuant to Class B where the installation would exceed 4 metres in height or be installed within the curtilage of a listed building. As with Class A, the development permitted by Class B is subject to conditions concerning amenity and removal once the development is no longer required.

Class J permits the installation or alteration of solar equipment on non-domestic premises including microgeneration solar thermal and PV equipment on a building, and other solar PV equipment on the roof. The interpretation provisions of Part 14 set out that "microgeneration" has the same meaning as in section 82(6) of the Energy Act 2004 which is the generation of electricity or production of heat of any plant the capacity of which does not exceed 50 kilowatts generation of electricity, or 45 kilowatts thermal in relation to the production of heat. To put that into perspective, the largest solar farm in the world has a total capacity of around 2.25 GW[42] or more than 2 million times the capacity of a microgeneration project.

---

[41] Defined by the GPDO as "solar PV or solar thermal equipment which is not installed on a building."

[42] Bhadla Solar Park, India

If solar PV equipment is installed on the roof of a non-domestic building pursuant to Class J(c)[43], then its capacity to generate electricity, together with any equipment installed under Class J(b)[44], must not exceed 1 megawatt.

Class K is the Class B equivalent for non-domestic premises, and permits the installation, alteration or replacement of stand-alone solar for microgeneration within the curtilage of a building other than a dwellinghouse or a block of flats. The parameters and conditions that follow will now be familiar and largely reflect those set out in the other classes of Part 14. In particular, and as with Class B, the surface area of the solar panels cannot exceed $9m^2$, or any dimension of the arrangement exceed 3m.

If the installation falls outside of the parameters of the permitted development right, then the installation could become an enforcement issue and an enforcement notice served pursuant to section 172 of TCPA 1990 if the LPA considers it to be "expedient" to issue the notice. If there is any doubt as to whether a particular project would be permitted development, section 192 of the TCPA 1990 provides a mechanism by which the lawfulness of a proposed use or development of land can be established. Guidance on lawful development certificates is set out online as part of the National Planning Practice Guidance ("NPPG") online resource[45].

Permitted development rights may not be available or may be restricted in respect of specified areas such as conservation areas, areas of outstanding natural beauty, and national parks; see Article 2(3), 2(4), Part 1 of Schedule 1.

---

43 Which relates to solar PV equipment on the roof of a building other than a dwellinghouse or a block of flats that is not covered by Class J(a), or Class J(b),.

44 Microgeneration solar PV equipment on a building

45 https://www.gov.uk/guidance/lawful-development-certificates

Larger Schemes

For larger solar developments not subject to the permitted development regime and which are less than 50MW, an application will need to be made under the provisions of the Town and Country Planning Act 1990 ("TCPA 1990"). For larger schemes with a generating capacity of more than 50MW, promoters will need to apply for development consent pursuant to the Planning Act 2008 ("PA 2008"). Development consent is required under the PA 2008 when the development is or forms part of a nationally significant infrastructure project ("NSIP"). NSIPs are defined in section 14(1)(a) of the PA 2008 to mean a project which consists of "the construction or extension of a generating station." Solar generating stations to which section 14(1)(a) relates are those that are within England, where its capacity is more than 50MW; see section 15(2)(c). The threshold for an NSIP in Wales is 350 megawatts up to which point, the decision rests with the Welsh Government under the Developments of National Significance ("DNS") Regime. If over 350MW, the project is determined by the UK Government as an NSIP.

The capacity that is referred to is the "generating capacity"[46] of the panels rather than the energy exported to the grid since that has to feed though an external inverter to convert the electricity from direct current ("DC") to alternating current ("AC") before a transformer steps-up the voltage for export.[47] Decisions are made by the Secretary of State of Business, Energy and Industrial Strategy following consideration of a report by an Examining Authority.

Only two Development Consent Orders ("DCO") have been granted for solar projects under the NSIP regime, and those decisions will be

---

46 https://www.gov.uk/guidance/consents-and-planning-applications-for-national-energy-infrastructure-projects#electricity-development-consents

47 Although Draft NPS EN-3 proposes that once the draft NPS is designated, for the purposes of the PA 2008, the combined capacity of the installed inverters (measured in AC) will be used for determining capacity, which will be 50MW (AC) in England, and 350MW (AC) in Wales.

explored below. Further schemes are currently in the process, including the Sunnica Energy Farm which was accepted on 16 December 2021 and the Longfield Solar Farm which was accepted for examination on 28 March 2022. However, it is expected that there will be many more applications in the system in due course given changes the proposed changes to the energy National Policy Statements which are addressed in Chapter 3.

Applications made pursuant to the TCPA 1990 are made to the relevant LPA, or LPAs if the application is a cross-boundary proposal. In two tier council areas, the relevant LPA will be the district council, but in certain instances, where the LPA has been designated for the purpose of section 62A of the TCPA 1990 application may be submitted to the Secretary of State. A LPA is designated where the Secretary of State considers that the LPA is not adequately performing its function of determining applications when assessed against published criteria.[48] There is only one current designation which came into force on 8 February 2022, and is in respect of Uttlesford District Council,

There are national information requirements set out in the Town and Country Planning (Development Management Procedure (England) (Order) 2015 and expanded upon in the NPPG[49] which set out the documentation and evidence that is required to be submitted as part of a planning application. In addition, individual LPAs should publish lists of their information requirements for applications for planning permission. National planning policy contained within the NPPF sets out at paragraph 44 that requirements should be kept to a minimum, reviewed every two years, and that only information that is relevant, necessary and material to the application in question should be required. Accordingly, the documentation that will need to be submitted can vary throughout the country.

---

48 https://www.gov.uk/government/publications/improving-planning-performance-criteria-for-designation

49 https://www.gov.uk/guidance/making-an-application

Decisions can be made by officers of the Council pursuant to delegated authority, or by Members of the Council sitting on the relevant committee. Depending on the adopted Scheme of Delegation which varies between LPAs, many applications, particularly those that are large and contentious will be determined by the LPA's Planning Committee of elected councillors. In some cases, the Secretary of State for Levelling Up, Housing and Communities will determine the application. Planning applications can be 'called in' by the Secretary of State if the application is particularly controversial or is nationally significant albeit not large enough to meet the PA 2008 definition.

Appeals pursuant to the TCPA 1990 will generally be determined by a planning inspector appointed on behalf of the Secretary of State, but again, there is a mechanism by which the Secretary of State can intervene in the process to make the decision; these are called 'recovered appeals.' The policy that is taken into consideration when a decision on whether to recover a planning appeal is made is contained within various Written Ministerial Statements[50]. If an appeal is recovered, the appeal is considered by a planning inspector, usually at a public planning inquiry, after which, the inspector will write a report that recommends how the appeal should be determined. The Secretary of State makes the decision having regard to that report but is under no obligation to agree with the inspector's recommendation.

Promoters of large-scale developments or developments in particularly sensitive locations should consider at an early stage the application of the Town and Country Planning (Environmental Impact Assessment) Regulations 2017 ("EIA Regulations") in relation to TCPA 1990 applications, or the Infrastructure Planning (Environmental Impact Assessment) Regulations 2017 for an application made under the PA 2008. Those matters are addressed further below.

---

50 https://www.gov.uk/government/collections/planning-applications-called-in-decisions-and-recovered-appeals#recovered-planning-appeals

CHAPTER THREE

THE ROLE OF LAW, POLICY AND GUIDANCE IN SOLAR DEVELOPMENT

Legislation

The law relevant to solar development has been touched on already throughout the first two chapters. Section 1 of the CCA Act 2008 sets a legally binding target that forms the basis for the UK's approach to climate change, and the requirement to achieve net zero carbon emissions by 2050. The CCA 2008 provides the overarching context for renewable and low carbon schemes that can make an important contribution to addressing climate change and assist with meeting the UK's targets.

Applications for NSIPs will be considered primarily in the context of the PA 2008 although large schemes may well require consents and licences under regimes other than the Planning Acts, for example, environmental permits pursuant to the Environmental Permitting (England and Wales) Regulations 2016 and a generation licence under the Electricity Act 1989.

National Policy Statements ("NPS") are produced and designated by government for the purpose of the PA 2008 following consultation and publicity, and they provide the frameworks within which Examining Authorities make their recommendations to the Secretary of State. There are a number of NPSs that relate to different types of infrastructure, and six in respect of energy development. In cases where there is a NPS in effect, section 104 of the PA 2008 requires that the Secretary of State must have regard to the NPS in relation to the development proposed and must decide the application in accordance with the NPS unless one of the circumstances in that section prevails. Those circumstances include that the proposals would lead to the United Kingdom being in breach of any of its international obligations, duty, law, or because the adverse impacts of the development would outweigh the benefits. Parallels can be drawn between the presumption in favour of the development plan for TCPA 1990 applications, and the status of NPSs in PA 2008 applications.

Where there is no relevant NPS as is presently the case with solar generation, section 105 of the PA 2008 applies. Solar generation is currently excluded from the scope of the Overarching National Policy Statement for Energy (EN-1) at paragraph 1.4.5 and the coverage of the NPS for Renewable Energy Infrastructure (EN-3) at paragraph 1.8, and so there is no designated NPS that has effect in relation to nationally significant solar energy development. Section 105 therefore requires that in deciding the application, the Secretary of State should have regard to any local impact report[51] ("LIR") any matter prescribed, and any other matters which the Secretary of State thinks are both important and relevant. Section 106 sets out the matter that may be disregarded when deciding an application, and that includes evidence which is:

(a) Vexatious or frivolous.

(b) Relates to the merits of the policy set out in the NPSs; or

(c) Relates to compensation for the compulsory acquisition of land or of an interest in or right over land.

The LIR that is submitted by local authorities pursuant to section 60 of the PA 2008 will usually set out relevant development plan policies, and supplementary planning documents ("SPDs"), but there is no requirement for the Secretary of State to determine the application in accordance with the development plan (unless material considerations indicate otherwise), unlike applications made pursuant to the TCPA

---

51 A local impact report or "LIR" gives details of the likely impact of the proposal on the authority's area; see PA 2008 section 60.

1990. Moreover, most development plans will not have been drafted with nationally significant energy development in mind, and so the application of local policies relating to much smaller renewables development, and development generally, has to be approached with some caution. However, the development plan is likely to be a relevant and even important consideration in the determination of the application and so both applicants and interested parties should consider relevant policies in their representations. Most development plans provide some support for renewable energy development, although it might be heavily caveated, and most local authorities have declared a climate emergency, which is important context in the promotion of solar schemes.

For applications made under the Town and Country Planning Act 1990, section 38(6) of the Planning and Compulsory Purchase Act 2004 ("PCPA 2004") and section 70(2) of the TCPA 1990 applications for planning permission be determined in accordance with the development plan, unless material considerations indicate otherwise. One of the key material considerations is the NPPF which is addressed further below, and which must also be taken into account when preparing development plans. Paragraph 2 of the NPPF also sets out that planning policies and decisions must reflect relevant international obligations and statutory requirements.

While the proper interpretation of planning policy is a matter of law for the court, the application of relevant policy and the weight to be given to it in decision taking is exclusively for the decision-taker. The courts have set out that planning policies are to be interpreted objectively by the court in accordance with the language used and in their proper context, and that a failure properly to understand and apply relevant policy will constitute a failure to have regard to a material consideration, or will amount to having regard to an immaterial consideration (see the judgment of Lord Reed in *Tesco Stores* [*Ltd.*] *v Dundee City Council* [2012] P.T.S.R. 983, at paragraphs 17 to 22).

Environmental Impacts of Solar Development

As set out in paragraph 3(a) of Schedule 2 of the EIA Regulations, industrial installations for the production of electricity where the area of development exceeds 0.5 hectares have the potential to give rise to significant effects on the environment. Unlike Schedule 1 development, Schedule 2 development is not automatically required to undergo Environmental Impact Assessment ("EIA"). If a development meets the applicable threshold and criteria set out in Schedule 2, the decision taker should consider whether it is likely to have significant effects on the environment having regard to the selection criteria set out in Schedule 3. That process if called "screening".

In most instances, it is prudent for applicants to seek a screening opinion from the relevant planning authority (the LPA or the Secretary of State) at an early stage in accordance with regulation 6 of the EIA Regulations. The production and submission of environmental information is time consuming and is required to meet with the requirements of Schedule 4 of the EIA Regulations. While much of the information required for inclusion in an Environmental Statement ("ES") will usually be produced to support a planning application in any event (e.g. landscape and visual impact assessment), there are elements of EIA that applicants wouldn't routinely include, such as information on the risk of major accidents and/or disaster.

If no screening decision is sought and made, and an ES isn't produced when the application is made, it may be required at a later stage. That could be when the decision taker carries out the screening exercise once an application is submitted or, if the project is appealed, the Secretary of State may make a screening direction of their own volition or if requested to do so in writing by any person[52]. Where development is EIA

[52] EIA Regulations, Regulation 5(6). A regulation 5(6) screening direction was made by the Secretary of State in respect of Appeal **APP/B3030/W/21/3279533** a month before the section 78 inquiry was due to open, giving the Appellant just weeks to produce an ES. The

development, then regulation 3 prohibits the grant of planning permission for that development unless an EIA has been carried out in respect of it. Applicants will therefore (usually) be given the opportunity to provide the information, but it can significantly slow the process down if not dealt with at an early stage and can cause procedural issues if the information needs to be produced and consulted upon within an appeal timetable.

It should be noted that the recent Levelling Up and Regeneration Bill ("LURB") proposes the replacement of the EIA and Strategic Environmental Assessment ("SEA") regimes with a new system of environmental assessment called 'Environmental Outcomes Reports.' The Government has been clear that post-Brexit, overall environmental protection should not be less than it currently is, but the reforms are designed to implement a clearer and simpler process than the one under the EIA Regulations.

A further consideration with utility scale solar development is the Conservation of Habitats and Species Regulations 2017 ("the Habitats Regulations") amended by the Conservation of Habitats and Species (Amendment) (EU Exit) Regulations 2019 which govern the assessment process that must be undertaken with respect to a development's implications for the national site network ("NSN") sites and Ramsar sites[53].

Special Areas of Conservation ("SACs") are sites which are designated because of a threat to the habitats or species which they contain and to provide increased protection to a variety of animals, plants and habitats of importance to biodiversity. A Special Protection Area ("SPA") is designated because it is an internationally important area for breeding,

---

consultation period extended beyond the inquiry sitting days, such that the inquiry formally closed a month after the inquiry to allow for full consideration of the ES.

53 A wetland site of international importance that is designated under the Ramsar Convention.

over-wintering and migrating birds. Together those sites make up the Natura 2000 network and are part of the NSN. Ramsar sites are wetlands of international importance, and many overlap with SACs and SPAs. Ramsar sites and proposed Ramsar sites together with potential SPAs, SACs and sites identified, or required as compensatory measures for adverse effects on habitats sites are given equal protection in the NPPF.[54]

Accordingly, if proposals could affect any of those protected site, the competent authority (the relevant planning authority, the relevant Minister, Welsh Ministers and Scottish Ministers) should carry out an assessment under the Habitats Regulations know as Habitats Regulations Assessment ("HRA"). Typically, the applicant will carry out what is known as a "shadow HRA" and provide the necessary information for the purposes of the assessment as well as conclusions on whether an Appropriate Assessment ("AA") is required, and if so, whether there would still be an adverse effect following mitigation.

The first stage in HRA is to screen the proposal and consider whether or not there is a risk of the proposals having a significant effect on the designated site on its own or in combination with other projects. At this stage, mitigation cannot be taken into account[55]. If the project is likely to have a significant effect on the site's conservation objectives, then the competent authority will need to carry out an AA that assesses the likely significant effects of a proposal on the integrity of the affected site and its conservation objectives, and the ways to avoid or mitigate any potential for an adverse effect on the integrity of the site.

If adverse effects cannot be avoided, it may still be possible for development to go ahead if certain requirements set out within the Habitats Regulations are met, the first of which is that there are no alternative solutions that would be less damaging to the European site;

---

[54] NPPF, paragraph 181

[55] *People Over Wind & Sweetman v. Coillte Teoranta* (C-323/17), and reflected in the NPPG https://www.gov.uk/guidance/habitats-regulations-assessments-protecting-a-european-site#screening

see regulation 64(1). It is also necessary to demonstrate that the development is required for imperative reasons of overriding public interest, and that necessary compensatory measures could be secured. In short, if such impacts can be avoided, they should be, and paragraph 182 of the NPPF makes clear that the presumption in favour of sustainable development will not apply where the plan or project (alone or in combination) is likely to have a significant effect on a habitats site unless an appropriate assessment has concluded that the plan or project will not adversely affect the integrity of the habitats site.

Policy for PA 2008 schemes

As set out above, solar energy development is currently excluded from the scope of the NPSs However, there are two important points. First, the fact that the NPSs do not explicitly refer to solar energy does not mean they are irrelevant in the determination of proposals for solar energy development, and parts of them may be relevant and even important in the consideration of those proposals. For example, overarching policy objectives set out in EN-1 are supportive of renewable energy generation and its essential role in improving energy security. Such statements, and the thrust of the NPSs are likely to be relevant and important.[56]

The second point is that in September 2021, following the publication of the Energy White Paper on 14 December 2020 in which the Government announced a review of the suite of energy NPSs, five draft NPSs were published for consultation. They include a new draft Overarching Energy NPS, and a new draft EN-3 on renewable energy. The consultation closed on 9 November 2021 and the NPSs are expected to be designated by summer of 2022, and so it is helpful to include a brief analysis of the draft documents insofar as they are relevant to solar

56 See for example, Little Crow Solar Park Report of the examining Authority §3.2.3-3.2.6, and the of the Secretary of State's decision letter §4.16-4.23

development, noting that the content of the final versions may change. In relation to the draft EN-1:

(i) Solar energy development now falls within the scope of EN-1. The draft explains that is has effect in relation to applications for energy development that are nationally significant under the Planning Act 2008 (§1.1.1) but that it may also be a material consideration in decision taking on applications under the TCPA 1990 "judged on a case by case basis..." §1.2.1. The same point is made in draft EN-3.

(ii) It confirms that there is an "urgent need" for new electricity generation (§3.3.20), and that solar is one of the lowest costs ways of generating electricity, and that a secure, reliable, affordable, net zero consistent system in 2050 is likely to be composed predominantly of wind and solar (§3.3.21).

(iii) Noting the intermittent natures of those technologies, the NPS also addresses the "key role" of storage in achieving net zero and providing flexibility in the energy system (§3.3.24). That is important since many solar schemes are co-located with battery energy storage systems either as a complimentary or a standalone project.

In respect of EN-3:

(i) The draft NPS anticipates a significant increase in low carbon electricity generation over the coming decades and acknowledges that renewable sources of energy are "an essential elements of the transition to net zero" (§1.1.1).

(ii) Policy in relation to solar farms starts from paragraph 2.47 by observing that solar is *"one of the most established renewable electricity technologies in the UK and the cheapest form of electricity generation worldwide."* The draft NPS notes that solar projects can be built quickly, benefit from improvements in panel efficiency and that large-scale solar is now, in some cases able to be deployed without reliance on subsidies.

(iii) Paragraph 2.48.7 addresses the previous disparity that has existed between solar energy development and other renewable technologies in respect of capacity thresholds. Solar panels generate electricity in direct current (DC) which is then fed into an external inverter that converts the electricity to alternating current (AC). Accordingly, there are two possible measurements for the capacity of a solar farm which is the capacity of the panels (DC) or the inverters (AC). Until now, the assessment has been assessed on DC generating capacity. All other forms of renewables are assessed on an AC basis, but once the draft NPS is designated, the capacity threshold for solar farms will also be considered on an AC basis. Practically this allows developers to over-install panels (relative to the energy to be exported) having regard to the intermittent nature of sunlight as a natural resource, as well as the degradation of panels over time.

(iv) While the draft EN-3 expresses a preference for the use of lower quality land for solar projects (brownfield and non-agricultural), the document explains that land type should not be the predominating factor in determining the suitability of the site location."[57] The draft also notes that solar development is not prohibited on sites that have good quality agricultural land (referred to in the NPPF as "best and most versatile agricultural land"), but that applicants should explain the choice of site.

(v) The policy set out further considerations including access, site layout design, impact on public rights of way, biodiversity and landscape and visual impacts. The section on project lifetimes recognises that solar panels typically have a design life of

[57] Paragraph 2.48.13

between 25 to 30 years, although many projects now seek temporary permission for 40 years, owing to more recent manufacturers' warranties in respect of panels. The policy expects that applicants will set out what would be decommissioned and removed from the stie at the end of its operational life, recognising that there may be some benefits in the retention of certain infrastructure including pathways though the site, and on-site substations. DCOs should set out a time-limit from first generation of electricity and should secure the decommissioning of the scheme.

Policy for TCPA 1990 schemes

In respect of TCPA 1990 applications, the NPPF sets out the Government's planning policies for England and its policies are a material consideration in planning decisions (para.218). The policies of the NPPF concern a range of planning considerations and should be read as a whole (para.3). The NPPF does not contain policies on nationally significant infrastructure projects, but it may still be relevant when considering such projects. It is likely to be an important material consideration in determining applications made pursuant to the TCPA 1990.

The NPPF sets out that the purpose of the planning system is to contribute to the achievement of sustainable development. The concept of sustainable development is summarised "as meeting the needs of the present without compromising the ability of future generations to meet their own needs."[58] It is expressed in the NPPF through the three overarching objectives which paragraph 8 explains are "interdependent and need to be pursued in mutually supportive ways (so that opportunities can be taken to secure net gains across each of the different

[58] Resolution 42/187 of the United Nations General Assembly

objectives)." The three objectives are economic, environmental, and social.

At the heart of the NPPF is the "presumption in favour of sustainable development." The operation of the presumption is set out at paragraph 11, with the first part relating to plan-making, and the second part relating to decision-taking. If development proposals accord with an up-to-date development plan, then paragraph 11(c) of the NPPF instructs decision takers to grant permission without delay, echoing the provisions of section 38(6). For a scheme to accord with the development plan it doesn't have to accord with every policy, or every part of every policy since the development plan should be read as a whole and it is not unusual for policies within a plan to pull in different directions. For example, a plan may promote low carbon energy sources, but also seek to protect the countryside where large scale energy projects are likely to be developed.[59] If schemes do not accord with the development plan, they may be refused unless material consideration indicate otherwise.

However, as set out above, the policies of the NPPF are a material consideration in planning decisions, and the application of the NPPF can affect the decision-making process, and the weight to be given to development plan policies that are out-of-date and/or which are inconsistent with the NPPF; see paragraph 219. Where there are no relevant development plan policies, or the most important policies for determining the application are out-of-date,[60] then the NPPF at paragraph 11(d) instructs that permission should be granted unless:

---

59 See discussion in *R (William Corbett) v. The Cornwall Council* [2020] EWCA 508 from para. 27 to 30

60 See discussion in *Bloor Homes East Midlands Ltd v, Secretary of State for Communities and Local Government* [2014] EWHC 754 (Admin) at para.45 for when individual policies might be out-of-date. In relation to when the most important policies may be regarded as out of date, see the discussion in *Wavendon Properties Ltd v Secretary of State for Housing, Communities and Local Government* [2019] P.T.S.R 2077 at paragraph 58

(i) Pursuant to paragraph 11(d)(i), the application of policies in the NPPF which protect areas or assets of particular importance such as Green Belt, National Parks, and irreplaceable habitats, provide a clear reason for refusing the development. The protected areas and assets to which this part relates are listed in footnote 7.

(ii) Alternatively, even if paragraph 11(d)(i) is not engaged, paragraph 11(d)(ii) instructs that permission should be refused where the adverse impacts of the scheme would significantly and demonstrably outweigh its benefits, when assessed against the policies in the NPPF as a whole. The phrase "when assessed against the policies in the NPPF as a whole" does not exclude consideration of development plan policies which will often inform the balancing exercise required under paragraph 11(d)(ii) and facilitate the assessment of adverse impact and benefits.[61]

Paragraph 11(d) is often referred to as "the tilted balance" because it tilts the balance in favour of the grant of planning permission as a policy mechanism to ensure sustainable development is granted permission even though it might be in conflict with the development plan.

The NPPF defines 'renewable and low carbon energy' in the glossary as including energy for heating and cooling as well as generating electricity. "Renewable energy covers those energy flows that occur naturally and repeatedly in the environment – from the wind, the fall of water, the movement of the oceans, from the sun and also from biomass and deep geothermal heat. Low carbon technologies are those that can help reduce emissions (compared to conventional use of fossil fuels)."

Paragraph 152 of chapter 14 which includes policies to meet the challenge of climate change, flooding and coastal change sets out that the

---

[61] *Gladman Developments Ltd v Secretary of State for Housing, Communities and Local Government* [2021] P.T.S.R 1450

planning system should "support the transition to a low carbon future in a changing climate", and "support renewable and low carbon energy and associated infrastructure." That support is not unqualified but does give decision-takers a clear steer as to how they should be approaching applications for solar development.

The section on planning for climate change encourages plans to help increase the use and supply of renewable and low carbon energy and heat, by providing a positive strategy for development, and to consider identifying suitable areas for renewable and low carbon energy sources (paragraph 155). Community-led initiatives for renewable energy are supported at paragraph 156 in which LPAs are instructed to support such initiatives, even where they are outside areas identified in local plans.

Importantly, paragraph 158 sets out that applications for renewable and low carbon development should not be required to demonstrate the overall need for renewable or low carbon energy, and that LPAs should recognise that even small-scale projects can provide a valuable contribution to cutting greenhouse gas emissions. The existence of the climate change crisis, and the need for renewable energy development is rarely contentious in applications and appeals, but if it becomes so, promoters of solar schemes need only refer to NPPF paragraph 158 which decisively answers the point.

Further, the NPPF sets out that decision-takers should approve applications where the impacts "are (or can be made) acceptable." The one exception to that is in respect of certain wind energy developments which have to meet the additional criteria set out in footnote 54. Paragraph 158 also requires that if suitable areas for renewable and low carbon energy have been identified in plans, then applications outside of those areas will need to demonstrate that the proposed location meets the criteria used in identifying suitable areas. There is however no blanket prohibition on renewable energy development outside of the suitable areas that have been identified, and so LPAs might not see the benefit of the exercise, which is likely to be time consuming and contentious, and will be subject to examination through the local plan process. Rather, it may be more beneficial for a LPA to simply identify the criteria against which renewable energy projects anywhere in its administrative area will be assessed.

It is worth noting that paragraph 151 in Chapter 13 'Green Belt' sets out that when located in the Green Belt, many renewable energy projects will comprise "inappropriate development". Inappropriate development is a concept associated with Green Belt policy and is harmful by definition in areas allocated as Green Belt. Inappropriate development should not be approved except in very special circumstances (paragraph 147). Very special circumstances will not exist unless "the potential harm to the Green Belt by reason of inappropriateness, and any other harm resulting from the proposal, is clearly outweighed by other considerations" (paragraph 148). However, paragraph 151 sets out that where renewable energy projects comprise inappropriate development, then very special circumstances "*may include the wider environmental benefits associated with increased production of energy from renewable sources.*" That is significant, since it is the only paragraph in the NPPF that seeks to define what considerations might amount to very special circumstances in respect of inappropriate development, and it serves to emphasise the need and support for renewable energy development in national policy.

National Planning Policy Guidance

The online guidance on renewable and law carbon energy was first published in 2014 (revised in 2015) and sits below national policy. It contains a chapter on renewable and low carbon energy "to help local councils in developing policies for renewable and low carbon energy and identifies the planning considerations."[62] The guidance sets out particular planning consideration that are relevant to proposals for solar development distinguishing between solar development relating to

[62] https://www.gov.uk/guidance/renewable-and-low-carbon-energy

buildings, and ground-mounted solar farms. In respect of the former, the factors to bear in mind include:

> *"the importance of siting systems in situations where they can collect the most energy from the sun;*
>
> *need for sufficient area of solar modules to produce the required energy output from the system;*
>
> *the effect on a protected area such as an Area of Outstanding Natural Beauty or other designated areas;*
>
> *the colour and appearance of the modules, particularly if not a standard design."*[63]

In respect of larger-scale solar farms, the particular planning considerations are listed as follows:

> *"encouraging the effective use of land by focussing large scale solar farms on previously developed and non agricultural land, provided that it is not of high environmental value;*
>
> *where a proposal involves greenfield land, whether (i) the proposed use of any agricultural land has been shown to be necessary and poorer quality land has been used in preference to higher quality land; and (ii) the proposal allows for continued agricultural use where applicable and/or encourages biodiversity improvements around arrays. See also a speech by the Minister for Energy and Climate Change, the Rt Hon Gregory Barker MP, to the solar PV industry on 25 April 2013 and written ministerial statement on solar energy: protecting the local and global environment made on 25 March 2015.*

---

63 Paragraph: 012 Reference ID: 5-012-20140306

that solar farms are normally temporary structures and planning conditions can be used to ensure that the installations are removed when no longer in use and the land is restored to its previous use;

the proposal's visual impact, the effect on landscape of glint and glare (see guidance on landscape assessment) and on neighbouring uses and aircraft safety;

the extent to which there may be additional impacts if solar arrays follow the daily movement of the sun;

the need for, and impact of, security measures such as lights and fencing;

great care should be taken to ensure heritage assets are conserved in a manner appropriate to their significance, including the impact of proposals on views important to their setting. As the significance of a heritage asset derives not only from its physical presence, but also from its setting, careful consideration should be given to the impact of large scale solar farms on such assets. Depending on their scale, design and prominence, a large scale solar farm within the setting of a heritage asset may cause substantial harm to the significance of the asset;

the potential to mitigate landscape and visual impacts through, for example, screening with native hedges;

the energy generating potential, which can vary for a number of reasons including, latitude and aspect."[64]

The reference to the speech by the then Minister for Energy and Climate Change in April 2013 and the highly emotive and frankly negative WMS on solar energy dated 25 March 2015 are interesting because they are

---

[64] Paragraph: 013 Reference ID: 5-013-20150327

arguably out-of-date and superseded by more recent policy (both draft and in force), and up-to-date government announcements and strategies which unequivocally support the delivery of large-scale solar schemes to achieve 70GW of installed capacity by 2035. It is not credible to suggest that the level of solar development anticipated could be accommodated on previously developed or non-agricultural land, and factors such as the availability of grid connection, absence of landscape designation and avoidance of harm to the historic landscape are all matters which need to be considered at site selection stage alongside the quality of the agricultural land. Moreover, draft NPS EN-3 now sets out that "where possible" schemes should utilise previously developed land but goes on to state that "land type should not be a predominating factor in determining the suitability of the site location."[65] If that sound and pragmatic approach is good enough for schemes over 50MW, it is difficult to see why it should not be so for smaller schemes.

At the local level there may be other policy and/or guidance documents relating to matters such as landscape sensitivity or capacity, the historic environment, or even specific information concerning renewable energy development to assist those involved in the process of making and determining applications. There will also be evidence-based documents that form a material consideration in the assessment of planning applications, but which do not set out specific policy or guidance. Applicants and LPAs should have regard to these documents in the course of their assessment of the proposed development. In considering the weight to be given to them, it will be relevant to consider the age of the document, whether it was published in the context of up-to-date evidence and information, whether its scope includes the assessment of solar development, and whether it has been superseded by later policy or guidance.

---

[65] At paragraph 2.48.13

CHAPTER FOUR

IMPACTS AND BENEFITS

This chapter explores the impacts and benefits that will arise in respect of most large-scale solar projects and how they can be assessed, managed and mitigated through the application and appeals processes. While the impacts and benefits will differ from scheme to scheme, large scale solar development will almost inevitably give rise to landscape character and visual impacts and is likely to give rise to harm to the historic environment since there are around 400,000 listed buildings in England, approximately 10,000 Conservation Areas, and almost 20,000 scheduled monuments. It is difficult to site any large-scale development without at least the potential for adverse impacts on a heritage asset either directly, or indirectly through a change in the setting. Similarly, many large-scale schemes will need to be sited in the open countryside, and the change from undeveloped greenfield land to land used as a solar farm will inevitably be regarded as harmful to at least the character of the site and possibly beyond, if the scheme can be perceived in the wider landscape or in combination with other solar projects.

Site Selection

Site selection is the first and possibly most important stage in the promotion of any development on land that is not allocated in a local plan. As set out above, the vast majority of LPAs will not have identified broad areas appropriate for renewable energy development, and even fewer plans (if any) will allocate sites specifically for solar development. A good scheme starts with a good site that is capable of accommodating the development with only limited impacts. Irradiance will be a key consideration for promoters of solar development, and it will also be necessary to consider the constraints set out below. The list is not intended to be exhaustive:

(i) **Policy designations.** Schemes should avoid undeveloped landscapes that are designated for their landscape quality and/or scenic beauty and those parts of their setting that make an important contribution to the designated landscape. These include Areas of Outstanding Natural Beauty, National Parks, and locally designated landscapes. Where that is not possible, serious consideration should be given to the justification for the proposed location, and any mitigation and enhancement that can be provided. Other planning policy designations may be relevant under this heading, including Green Belt, policies designed to prevent coalescence, and general countryside policies. All will require careful consideration in the planning arguments made in support of a scheme.

(ii) **Topography of the site, enclosure and visibility.** The more contained a site is, the more likely it is that landscape character impacts will be capable of being mitigated. Conversely, schemes in prominent landscapes with sloping and/or elevated topography generally have greater propensity to give rise to adverse landscape effects.

(iii) **Proximity to public rights of way ("PROW").** There is a large PROW network throughout the UK, and schemes will have to ensure that the PROW can be retained where possible, and that the visual impacts of the scheme on users can be mitigated. Users of PROW are generally regarded as high sensitivity receptors in respect of new development, because the landscape tends to be part of the experience of the user. Consideration will have to be given to their experience and how that might change. Applicants might want to consider extending the footpath network throughout land over which they have control, siting panels further away from the PROW or incorporating additional planting to filter views. Those involved in the process may also want to consider the nature of the footpath(s) to be affected, the length of the route, specific viewpoints, and whether the experience of using the route is or can be replicated in areas not affected by proposed development.

(iv) **Proximity to residential dwellings.** There is no right to a view that is protected in planning law or policy, but there does come a point where the impact of development on a dwelling or dwellings can be of such a magnitude so as to affect the residential amenity of the occupiers of a property, and make it an unattractive and unsatisfactory place to live[66]. There are no hard and fast rules as to when the threshold is crossed, it will be a matter of judgement in every case. It may be necessary to carry out a Residential Visual Amenity Assessment in accordance with the technical guidance of the Landscape Institute to better understand the interaction between the proposed site and nearby dwellings. The assessment should be carried out and produced following professional input from landscape and planning professionals. Glint and glare associated with the scheme will also need to be considered.

(v) **The historic environment.** Applicants will need to consider the proximity of the site to designated[67] as well as non-designated heritage assets[68], and whether or not the scheme will impact on the setting of those assets or the assets directly. A heritage impact assessment should be carried out where impacts may arise, and proposed development should avoid substantial

66 Often referred to as "the Lavender test" following the decision of Inspector Lavender in the Enifer Downs windfarm appeal decision APP/X2220/A/08/2071880, 28 April 2009

67 Defined in the NPPF as a World Heritage Site, Scheduled Monument, Listed Building, Protected Wreck Site, Registered Park and Garden, Registered Battlefield or Conservation Area designated under the relevant legislation.

68 Defined in the NPPF as heritage assets of archaeological interest, which are demonstrably of equivalent significance to scheduled monuments, and should be considered subject to the policies for designated heritage assets.

harm or total loss of designated heritage assets since national policy imposes a high threshold for the justification of such harm (see NPPF paragraph 201). It may not be possible to avoid causing less than substantial harm ("LTSH") which is addressed further below. It should be remembered that the term "heritage asset" can include below ground archaeology, and that buried heritage assets can still have an above ground setting that requires preservation.

(vi) **Ecological interests.** Early advice should be sought from an ecological expert to understand whether there are any ecological constraints on or around a particular site that might restrict its development potential. The range of potential interests is vast, and assessment might be required of particular species, habitats, or other interactions with nearby protected sites. Applicants will want to pay specific attention to paragraph 180 of the NPPF which sets out policy in relation to biodiversity, designated sites, and irreplaceable habitats. Wholly exceptional reasons will be required to justify the loss or deterioration of irreplaceable habitats albeit nationally significant infrastructure projects are listed as a potential justification at footnote 63 where the public benefits of the projects outweigh the loss or deterioration of the habitats. It should also be noted that solar farms have the potential to provide very significant biodiversity enhancements, and this should be assessed and built into the scheme at an early stage.

(vii) **Agricultural land value.** The value of best and most versatile agricultural land (defined in the NPPF as land in grade 1, 2 and 3a of the Agricultural Land Classification) is recognised in national policy. Promoters should consider the value of the land, and what is likely to happen to it as a result of the construction of the scheme and over the lifetime of the development. National guidance sets out that where a proposal involves greenfield land that local authorities consider "*whether (i) the proposed use of any agricultural land has been shown to be* *necessary and poorer quality land has been used in preference to higher quality land; and (ii) the proposal allows for continued agricultural use where applicable and/or encourages biodiversity improvements around arrays."*[69] Unlike other permanent development, solar development does not lead to the "loss" of agricultural land save for small elements of permanent infrastructure such as substations. Depending upon what practices are employed, the land could still be used for food production (animal grazing), and a break in intensive arable farming can enhance the soil resource ready for use when the solar farm is decommissioned. Notwithstanding that, there may still be an argument for retaining the best agricultural land in productive arable use which is not possible alongside a solar farm.

Considering Impacts

If the site selection process demonstrates that accommodating solar development is technically feasible without overriding harm, then applicants should consider the detailed design of the scheme and how any residual impacts can be mitigated. The most common impacts that are likely to arise are landscape and visual impacts, and harm to the historic environment and so they are worth considering in more detail.

---

69 https://www.gov.uk/guidance/renewable-and-low-carbon-energy. The online guidance also refers to a speech by the then Minister for Energy and Climate Change in April 2013 and a WMS on solar energy dated 25 March 2015 which could be argued to be superseded by more recent policy both draft and in force, and up-to-date government announcements and strategies which unequivocally support the delivery of large-scale solar schemes.

Landscape and Visual Impacts

It is almost inevitable that large scale solar farms will give rise to landscape and visual effects, and that is recognised in the Draft NPS EN-1[70]. Minimising those impacts begins with site selection. A great site would be one that is previously developed, and where its development for solar energy could even enhance the local character. However, there are few brownfield sites of the size necessary to accommodate utility scale solar development, and so a good undeveloped site will generally be well enclosed with existing boundary vegetation with the potential for panels and associated infrastructure to be screened with additional planting. Sloping and rolling topography that is crossed by a large number of PROW will be more challenging since the development will be visible over a wider area, and more difficult to screen, even over the long term.

A landscape and visual impact assessment ("LVIA") should be carried out by a suitably qualified landscape professional at the early stages of the scheme. The LVIA should be undertaken in accordance with the Landscape Institute's Guidelines for Landscape and Visual Impacts Assessment, now in its third edition, and that will assess the sensitivity of the landscape having regard to the site and its landscape context, and the impacts of the scheme having regard to published landscape character assessments (national and local). The assessment should consider the short, medium and long-term effects of the scheme having regard to existing and proposed mitigation, which may be negative, neutral or even beneficial where additional planting enhances the structure of the landscape and contributes to the landscape resource.

Certain landscapes which are important for their landscape value and beauty require special consideration and may engage particular planning policies. For example, national policy contained within the NPPF at paragraph 177 sets out that applications for major development[71] should

---

[70] Paragraph 5.10.9

[71] NPPF footnote 60 sets out that for the purposes of paragraphs 176 and 177, "whether a proposal is 'major development' is a matter for the decision

be refused in AONBs and National Parks other than in exceptional circumstances, and where the development is in the public interest. Three further criteria are provided to assist in consideration of such applications, including:

(i) The need for the development, (which applicants are not required to demonstrate for solar energy), and the impact of approving or refusing the proposal on the local economy.

(ii) The cost of and scope for developing outside of the designated area, or meeting the need in some other way; and

(iii) The detrimental effects on the area, and the extent to which those impacts could be moderated.

In all circumstances "great weight" should be given to conserving and enhancing landscape and scenic beauty in National Parks, the Broads and AONBs, in accordance with paragraph 176 of the NPPF. Sites that are not nationally designated may still benefit from protection under paragraph 174(a) and (b) of the NPPF, which seeks to protect and enhance valued landscapes (in a manner commensurate with their statutory status or identified quality in a development plan) and requires that that planning decisions contribute to the enhance of the natural environment by "recognising the intrinsic character and beauty of the countryside…". The language of "recognising" is distinct from "protecting" and "enhancing", and thus ordinary countryside achieves the lowest level of protection. Nonetheless, impacts on all landscapes will have to be explored, and it should not be assumed that all undesignated countryside is equally capable of accommodating new solar development, or that all impacts will be acceptable in undesignated countryside because of the imperative to deliver renewable energy development.

---

maker, taking into account its nature, scale and setting, and whether it could have a significant adverse impact on the purposes for which the area has been designated or defined."

Visual impacts are distinct from landscape character impacts and should be assessed separately. Where there will be impacts on highly sensitive receptors, applicants should seek to mitigate those impacts through additional planting, pulling back or removing panels from certain parts of the site, and by providing new rights of way where possible so that users have an alternative route.

Impacts on the historic environment

There are overlapping protections in respect of some heritage assets. Section 66 of the Planning (Listed Buildings and Conservation Areas) Act 1990 ("PLBCAA 1990") places a statutory duty on decision takers in respect of listed buildings to have "special regard to the desirability of preserving the building or its setting or any features of special architectural or historic interest which it possesses" and section 72 requires that "special attention shall be paid to the desirability of preserving or enhancing the character or appearance" of conservation areas. The nature of the duty is the same in both sections despite the slight difference in wording.[72] Section 72 is not engaged unless the proposal is within the conservation area whereas section 66 is only engaged where development is within the setting of the listed building. However, the setting of conservation areas and all other heritage assets is also protected by the NPPF; see paragraph 200. The NPPF at paragraph 199 requires that "great weight" should be given to the conservation of all heritage assets when considering development proposals.

Setting is defined in the NPPF as:

> *"The surroundings in which a heritage asset is experienced. Its extent is not fixed and may change as the asset and its surroundings evolve. Elements of a setting may make a positive or negative contribution to the significance of an asset, may*

[72] *Barnwell Manor Wind Energy Limited v. East Northamptonshire District Council* [2014] EWCA Civ 137 at [16]

affect the ability to appreciate that significance or may be neutral."[73]

As set out in Historic England's guidance[74] on setting – to which regard should be had when performing a setting assessment as part of a Heritage Impacts Assessment ("HIA") – setting is not a heritage asset, its value is in what is contributes to the significance (the value and heritage interest) of a heritage asset. The significance of a heritage asset can be diminished through development in its setting, even when there is no direct effect on the asset itself. Similarly, development in an asset's setting may have no effect at all on the significance of an asset and the ability to appreciate it, and in some instances, there may also the potential for enhancement which leads to a positive outcome for the asset.

There is a significant body of case law in respect of heritage matters that can be summarised as follows:

(i) "Preserving" means doing no harm: see *South Lakeland District Council v Secretary of State for the Environment* [1992] 2 AC 141, per Lord Bridge at page 150.

(ii) Parliament in enacting section 66(1) intended that the desirability of preserving the settings of listed buildings should not simply be given careful consideration by the decision-maker for the purpose of deciding whether there would be some harm, but should be given "considerable importance and weight" when the decision-maker carries out the balancing

---

[73] Setting is not statutorily defined, and does not lend itself to precise definition (see *R. (on the application of Williams) v Powys County Council* [2017] EWCA Civ 427, at paragraphs 53 to 58. Identifying the extent of the setting will always be a matter of fact and planning judgment for the decision-maker. And as Sullivan L.J. said in *R. (on the application of The Friends of Hethel Ltd.) v South Norfolk District Council* [2011] 1 W.L.R. 1216,

[74] https://historicengland.org.uk/images-books/publications/gpa3-setting-of-heritage-assets/

exercise, per Sullivan LJ in *Barnwell Manor Wind Energy Limited v. East Northamptonshire District Council* [2014] EWCA Civ 137 at [24].

(iii) The statutory duties apply with particular force to assets of the highest significance[75], and is reduced, although not removed where the harm is less than substantial harm ("LTSH") within the meaning of the NPPF paragraph 201; *Barnwell Manor* at [28]. It follows that a finding of LTSH is not to be equated with a less than substantial objection to the grant of planning permission; *Barnwell Manor* at [29].

(iv) Where harm is caused to a heritage asset, even if that harm is LTSH within the meaning of the NPPF paragraph 201, there is "strong presumption" against the grant of planning permission; *Barnwell Manor* at [23].

(v) The approach to conserving and enhancing the historic environment within the NPPF corresponds with the duty in section 66 of the PLBCAA 1990; *Jones v. Mordue* [2015] EWCA Civ 1243 per Sales LJ at [28]. While that case concerned section 66 of the PLBCAA 1990, the same proposition would seem to apply in respect of section 72 too.

(vi) Although the statutory duty requires special regard to be paid to the desirability of not harming the setting of a listed building, that cannot mean that any harm, however minor, would necessarily require planning permission to be refused. The statutory duty does not require that planning permission must be refused: "*The duty to accord "considerable weight" to the desirability of avoiding harm does not mean that any harm, however slight, must outweigh any benefit, however great, or that*

[75] Defined in NPPF paragraph 200 as scheduled monuments, protected wreck sites, registered battlefields, grade I and II* listed buildings, grade I and II* registered parks and gardens, and World Heritage Sites

all harms must be treated as having equal weight. The desirability of avoiding a great harm must be greater than that of avoiding a small one. The desirability of avoiding harm to a high category heritage asset must be greater than that of avoiding a similar harm to a less important asset." *Palmer v Herefordshire Council* [2016] EWCA Civ 1061 affirming the judgment of HHJ David Cooke in the court below at [34].

(vii) In *Catesby Estates Ltd. v. Steer* [2018] EWCA Civ 1697, Lindblom LJ set down three general principles at [28] – [29] when considering the setting of a heritage asset and the impact of a proposed development upon it:

(1) It is necessary for a decision taker to understand and identify the setting, even if that is difficult, in order to perform the statutory obligation to have special regard to the desirability of preserving the setting.

(2) The setting of a heritage asset will be a matter of planning judgement having regard to the particular facts and circumstances as well as relevant policy, guidance and advice. The experience of a heritage asset is not limited to what can be seen. Other relationships might be important.

(3) Whether development in the setting of a heritage asset will harm its significance and how that bears on the overall planning balance are matters for the planning judgement of the decision-taker. As stated by Lord Carnwath in *Hopkins Homes Ltd. v Secretary of State for Communities and Local Government* [2017] 1 W.L.R. 1865 (at paragraph 25) "*the courts should respect the expertise of the specialist planning inspectors, and start at least from the presumption that they will have understood the policy framework correctly*".

Any harm to a designated heritage asset requires "clear and convincing justification".[76] Where development gives rise to LTSH, paragraph 202 of the NPPF requires that the harm should be weighed against the "public benefits" of the proposals which are defined in the PPG in the following way:

> *"… anything that delivers economic, social or environmental objectives as described in the National Planning Policy Framework (paragraph 8). Public benefits should flow from the proposed development. They should be of a nature or scale to be of benefit to the public at large and not just be a private benefit. However, benefits do not always have to be visible or accessible to the public in order to be genuine public benefits, for example, works to a listed private dwelling which secure its future as a designated heritage asset could be a public benefit."*[77]

Accordingly, a benefit does not have to be a specific "heritage benefit" to be weighed in the balance, and the provision of renewable energy that contributes to climate change objectives is undoubtedly a public benefit.

If the proposal gives rise to substantial harm, or total loss of significance of a designated heritage asset, then consent should be refused unless it can be demonstrated that the harm is "necessary" to achieve substantial public benefits, or all of the criteria (a) to (d) of paragraph 201 of the NPPF apply, including that no viable use of the heritage asset itself can be found in the medium term that will enable it conservation. Therefore, there is a high bar for causing substantial harm, or total loss of a designated heritage.

---

[76] NPPF, paragraph 199

[77] https://www.gov.uk/guidance/conserving-and-enhancing-the-historic-environment, Paragraph: 020 Reference ID: 18a-020-20190723

The nature of "substantial harm" was discussed in *Bedford Borough Council v. Secretary of State for Communities and Local Government* [2012] EWHC 344 with Jay J providing the following definition at [25]:

> *"Plainly in the context of physical harm, this would apply in the case of demolition or destruction, being a case of total loss. It would also apply to a case of serious damage to the structure of the building. In the context of non-physical or indirect harm, the yardstick was effectively the same. One was looking for an impact which would have such a serious impact on the significance of the asset that its significance was either vitiated altogether or very much reduced."*

While that formulation has for some time been regarded as a "test", the court in *London Historic Parks And Gardens Trust v Minister of State for Housing & Anor* [2022] EWHC 829 (Admin) eschewed the idea that *Bedford* could be regarded as authority for any particular threshold:

> *"53. Accordingly, read as a whole and in context, Jay J's judgment does not import a test of 'draining away' to the test of substantial harm. He was not seeking to impose a gloss on the term. The judgment in Bedford accords with the approach stated by the Senior President of Tribunals at [74] in Bramshill. It is clear from cases like Tesco v Dundee [2012] UKSC 13; R(Samuel Smith) v North Yorkshire County Council [2020] UKSC 3; Bramshill and others, that a word like 'substantial' in the NPPF means what it says and any attempt to impose a gloss on the meaning of the term has no justification in the context of the NPPF. The policy framework and guidance provide a steer that relevant factors include the degree of impact, the significance of the heritage asset under scrutiny and its setting. It is not appropriate to treat comments made by a Judge assessing the reasoning of an individual decision maker, when applying the test of 'substantial harm' to the circumstances before him/her, as creating a gloss or additional meaning to the test."*

The correct approach is set out in the Court of Appeal's judgment in *City & County Bramshill Limited v Secretary of State* [2021] 1 WLR 5761 per Lindblom LJ at [74]:

> *"... What amounts to "substantial harm" or "less than substantial harm" in a particular case will always depend on the circumstances. Whether there will be such "harm", and, if so, whether it will be "substantial", are matters of fact and planning judgment. The NPPF does not direct the decision-maker to adopt any specific approach to identifying "harm" or gauging its extent. It distinguishes the approach required in cases of "substantial harm ... (or total loss of significance ...)" (paragraph 195) from that required in cases of "less than substantial harm" (paragraph 196). But the decision-maker is not told how to assess what the "harm" to the heritage asset will be, or what should be taken into account in that exercise or excluded. The policy is in general terms. There is no one approach, suitable for every proposal affecting a "designated heritage asset" or its setting."*

The NPPF at paragraph 203 has regard to a further category of harm, and that is harm to non-designated heritage assets, which should be taken into account in determining the application, having regard to the scale of harm and the loss of significance of the asset. Commensurate with their status, harm to a non-designated heritage asset is unlikely to attract the same weight as harm to a designated asset.

In considering harm to heritage assets, it should be remembered that heritage assets generally have a long lifespan. Most have been around for many generations and will endure long after the decommissioning of solar development, even if the temporary permission lasts for forty years. Solar development may occupy a period in the lifespan of a heritage asset but is unlikely to have a defining impact on its long-term significance which will (in most cases) be completely restored at the end of the temporary permission.

Providing Benefits

In the context of the climate change emergency, the urgent need to reduce greenhouse gas emissions, and given the international and national support for renewable energy development, the biggest benefit arising from solar energy development is the contribution it can make to tackling climate change and assisting in the transition towards a net zero future.

However, solar development can give rise to additional benefits, notably in respect of biodiversity, and through the provision of additional landscaping and planting that can remain as a positive legacy of the scheme post decommissioning. Applicants should consider what additional benefits can be provided as part of the proposals, especially where there are unavoidable impacts on interests of high sensitivity.

By way of example, solar development is exceptionally well placed to deliver significant biodiversity net gain. It is well acknowledged that there has been a significant decline in biodiversity over the last 50 years, with the loss and degradation of much of the UK's wildlife-rich habitats and species.[78] The Environment Act 2021 ("The Environment Act") received Royal Assent on 9 November 2021 and provides a new framework for environmental governance following the UK's departure from the European Union; it seeks to improve the environment and halt the decline in species abundance by 2030. Among other measures, the Environment Act mandates biodiversity net gain though the planning system and requires a 10% increase in biodiversity after development compared to the level before. The requirement applies to NSIPs as well as development permitted pursuant to the TCPA 1990 and is likely to come into force in 2023.

Solar development is well placed to give rise to very significant biodiversity net gain over the lifetime of the scheme because of the size

[78] DEFRA, 'Nature recovery green paper: protected sites and Species,' March 2022

and nature of the development. Solar panels sit on rather than in the land, meaning that existing planting can for the most part be protected and enhanced, and the soil resource is still available for use. There is often the opportunity to change arable land, which may have limited biodiversity, into species rich grassland, which scores favourably when assessed using the biodiversity metric. Hedgerows can be restored, and new planting provided which has the dual benefit of screening the development and enhancing the landscape structure and green corridors throughout the site. Drainage and flood risk mitigation can lead to the creation of important wetland habitat. Land within the red line of the application, or adjacent to the proposal may be given over to and managed entirely for biodiversity enhancement. It is not unusual to see solar schemes achieve well over 50% biodiversity net gain, which is substantial.

Applicants may choose to explore the provision of further benefits through consultation with local communities and councils, and they should pay special attention to any neighbourhood, parish or village plans or guides. There may, for example be some need within the community for additional green space that can be provided as part of the scheme and would be regarded as a benefit of the proposals. However, applicants and decision-takers should be aware of attempts to buy or sell a planning permission through the imposition of planning conditions and obligations and LPAs should only regard as a material consideration those benefits which meet a planning purpose (relating to the character of the land) and are fairly and reasonably related to the development permitted, also know, as the *Newbury*[79] criteria.

In *R(on the application of Wright) v Resilient Energy Severndale Ltd & Forest of Dean District Council* [201] UKSC 53 Resilient Energy Severndale Ltd ("RES") applied and secured planning permission for a single wind turbine. As part of the application, RES proposed that the turbine would be erected and operated by a community benefit society and that an annual donation would be made to a local community fund

---

[79] *Newbury District Council v Secretary of State for the Environment* [1981] AC 578

based on a proportion of the society's turnover. The contribution was secured by condition and taken into account as a material consideration. In dismissing RES's appeal, the Supreme Court held at [44] that the community benefits promised by RES did not satisfy the Newbury criteria and so were not a material consideration. The financial contribution was not provided for any proper planning purpose and did not fairly and reasonably relate to the development in question. Instead, it was said to have been proffered as a "general inducement to the Council to grant planning permission…". The planning permission was therefore quashed over four years after it was granted.

Accordingly, applicants should avoid, and LPAs should not require the provision of benefits which are not justified in local or national policy, and which do not otherwise satisfy the *Newbury* criteria.

CHAPTER FIVE

APPLICATIONS AND APPEALS PURSUANT TO THE TCPA 1990

Applications

As set out in Chapter 2, applications for solar energy development that are not permitted development, and which have a generating capacity of less than 50MW should be made pursuant to the Town and Country Planning Act. Applicants may wish to enter pre-application discussions with the LPA to understand how officers are likely to consider a proposal, what information should be submitted with the application, and whether an alternative scheme would be more likely to get planning permission. LPAs can only require information that is:

(i) reasonable having regard, in particular, to the nature and scale of the proposed development; and

(ii) about a matter which it is reasonable to think will be a material consideration in the determination of the application.[80]

Applicants and LPAs should also explore whether the proposal is likely to be EIA development, so that environmental information can be produced and consulted on as part of the application process.

Article 15 of The Town and Country Planning (Development Management Procedure) (England) Order 2015 ("DMPO") requires LPAs to publicise an application for planning permission with special requirements for EIA development. Article 18 of the DMPO requires the LPA to consult with specified consultees on certain planning applications

---

80 See section 62 (4A) of the Town and Country Planning Act 1990

prior to determination. For example, if development is likely to affect the site of a scheduled monument, battlefield, or Grade I or II* registered park or garden, then Historic England must be consulted. The relevant information is contained within Schedule 4 of the DMPO. Changes can be made to the application before it is determined by the LPA, but if that is the case, it may be necessary to reconsult on the updated information. Further guidance is contained within he NPPG under the section headed 'Making an application.'[81]

If the LPAs response is negative, and the application is refused then applicants may choose to appeal pursuant to section 78 of the TCPA 1990 but should take early advice from counsel on the prospects of success, mode of appeal, and how best to address the reasons for refusal. Similarly, LPAs should instruct a barrister early on in the process for advice on how best to defend an appeal, or whether it should be defended at all, particularly where a refusal is contrary to officer recommendation.

Amending the scheme

It may be that the scheme can and should be amended through the appeal process in response to the reasons for refusal, but applicants should be careful to ensure that if amendments proposed, then further consultation is undertaken in accordance with the "Wheatcroft principles"[82] and the guidance in the Planning Inspectorate's Good Practice Advice Note 09. Whether or not amendments to the scheme will be accepted is at the discretion of the planning inspector but the main criterion upon which that judgement will be exercised is fairness to all interested parties and *"whether the development is so changed that to grant it would be to deprive*

81 https://www.gov.uk/guidance/making-an-application#changes-after-validation-of-an-application

82 Which emerge from *Bernard Wheatcroft v. Secretary of State for the Environment and Another* (1982) 43 P. & C.R. 233

those who should have been consulted on the changed development of the opportunity of such consultation…"[83]

Accordingly, if changes are to be made to a scheme, even if they do not change the red line for development, the description of development, or have a significant effect on the impacts of the scheme, it is best practice to consult on those changes when an appeal is made so that all interested parties, statutory and non-statutory consultees can consider them and make their submissions accordingly. The changes and the reasons for them should be straightforwardly explained in one document and accompanied by plans where appropriate. Sufficient time should then be given for those consulted to make their comments. Other documents supporting the scheme may need to be updated by way of addenda to consider the amended scheme, such as landscape and visual appraisals, or environmental impact assessments.

Appeals

Insofar as it is relevant, section 78 provides that appeals can be made where a LPA refuses an application for permission or grants it subject to conditions, or has failed to determine the application within the relevant period.[84] Most planning appeals must be received within 6 months of the date on the decision notice.

There are three modes of appeal: written representations, hearings, and public inquiries. The majority of appeals are determined by written representations but that will seldom be an appropriate mode of appeal for large scale solar energy. Hearings and Inquiries give greater opportunity to explore the evidence, and to make legal submissions. Appeals conducted in person also provides parties with the chance to add to their written cases in response to points made by the other parties.

---

83 Ibid., per Forbes J at p.241

84 8 weeks for non-major applications, 13 weeks for major applications or 16 weeks for applications subject to an environmental impact assessment

Inquiries allow for the formal examination of evidence, and the rigour of the process – including the requirement to agree common ground, and exchange proofs of evidence – means that parties' cases are often more focused by the time the inquiry opens. While the statistics change from year to year, approximately 30% of all appeals are allowed with greater success for appellants following the inquiry procedure than either of the other two modes of appeal. An Appellant seeking an Inquiry, is required to inform the LPA and the Inspectorate at least 10 working days before submitting a planning appeal.

Notwithstanding that general position, the decision as to the mode of appeal ultimately rests with the Planning Inspectorate having regard to the published criteria in Annexe K of the Planning Inspectorate's detailed Procedural Guide to Planning Appeals[85] ("the Procedural Guide"). Accordingly, appellants and LPAs should carefully consider the criteria when considering the mode of appeal and justify their position accordingly. Larger schemes with several reasons for refusal and significant public interest are more likely to be determined through the public inquiry process than less controversial schemes where the only objection is landscape impact (for example).

Written Representations are governed by the Town and Country Planning (Appeals) (Written Representations Procedure) (England) Regulations 2009. Hearings are governed by the Town and Country Planning (Hearings Procedure) (England) Rules 2000, and inquiries by the Town and Country Planning Appeals (Determination by Inspectors) (Inquiries Procedure) (England) Rules 2000. Detailed guidance concerning the process, timetable, and required documents is contained within the Inspectorate's procedural guide which was last updated in April 2022, and which is reviewed annually.

---

[85] https://www.gov.uk/government/publications/planning-appeals-procedural-guide/procedural-guide-planning-appeals-england#annexe-k-criteria-for-determining-the-procedure-for-planning-listed-building-enforcement-hazardous-substances-advertisement-and-discontinuance-notice-appeals

Members of the public can take part in all modes of appeal and can formally participate as a "rule 6" party at inquiries. A party with rule 6 status can play a full role in the inquiry process, call evidence, cross examine, and is entitled to make opening and closing submissions in the same way as the Appellant and the LPA. A rule 6 party must also abide by the procedural rules as to the nature and timing of evidence and must not behave unreasonably in the process. Rule 6 parties are not bound by the reasons for refusal and may raise additional or alternative objections to a scheme. However, objections that are focused on disagreement with national policy, and the need for renewable energy will not succeed since those matters are for policy makers not planning inspectors.

Inquiries will generally take place over multiple days and parties will generally be legally represented although legal representation is not mandatory, and rule 6 parties will seldom instruct a legal representative. It would be highly unusual for an appellant or LPA not to be legally represented. A Case Management Conference ("CMC") is held prior to an inquiry to deal with procedural matters such as the length of the inquiry, the deadlines for submission of evidence, and the main issues for consideration. Hearings are generally shorter and a maximum of two days. It is becoming increasingly common for parties (especially appellants) to be legally represented by an advocate at hearings.

The main parties should instruct experts early on in the process and focus on the reasons for refusal. If there is a Rule 6 party, then the Appellant will need to be prepared to call additional evidence to respond to points which may go beyond the scope of the reasons for refusal. Appellants should also be careful to address points that are raised by other parties to the Inquiry either orally or in writing[86]. All parties should engage in the

[86] *London Historic Parks And Gardens Trust v Minister of State for Housing & Anor* [2022] EWHC 829 (Admin) at [112]-[129] where a decision was quashed on the basis of a point that was put before the inquiry "in modest fashion" via a third party written representation.

process of agreeing common ground to narrow the issues as far as possible.

The planning appeal regime is generally a "no costs regime" in that parties are expected to bear their own costs. The exception to that is where one party behaves unreasonably, and that behaviour causes another party to incur unnecessary or wasted expense in the appeal process. The behaviour can relate to procedural matters, or substantive issues concerning the merits of the appeal. Inspectors also have the ability to initiate an award of costs, even if no party has made a costs application, although the parties involved will be given the chance to make submissions as part of that process.

The appeal process concludes with the issuing of a decision letter from either the Secretary of State (if the appeal has been recovered) or an inspector.

Appeal Decisions

There are only a few recent appeal decisions for large scale solar development, albeit there are many appeals now in the pipeline. Most new solar development is granted permission locally by the relevant LPAs, and this book does not seek to find any trends or patterns among those decisions which are unlikely to be very persuasive in an appeal process unless the relevant decision is for solar development in the same area, applying the same policies in the same context.

While appeal decisions will turn on the specific facts of each case, especially the landscape and visual context and proximity to heritage assets, where general principles emerge, they may be useful for parties to raise as a material consideration for other decision takers to take into account. Older appeal decisions should be viewed with some caution, since they are unlikely to have been arrived at in the context of more recent unequivocal support for solar energy development at the national level.

In the past year there have been three decisions for solar development pursuant to the TCPA 1990. The first appeal decision[87] was for the construction of a solar park on a 62 hectare site in Hinckley and Bosworth Borough to generate approximately 35MW and was considered at a hearing. The site is located close to the Registered Battle of Bosworth Battlefield, which staged a defining moment in English history, and is a heritage asset of the highest significance. The Battle of Bosworth marked the last significant battle of the War of Roses and is the location where Richard III died, signalling a dynastic change between the House of Plantagenet and the House of Tudor.

The parties agreed that the scheme would give rise to LTSH to the Battlefield, principally arising from the impact of views to and from the Battlefield, and the loss of experience for observers of the landscape of the events of August 1485, over 500 years ago. The Inspector found that the public benefits of the scheme which included sufficient clean energy to power 10,500 homes, and economic benefits of around £35 million were insufficient to outweigh the LTSH which would "*deprive future generations of being able to understand and experience the events leading to and of the battle itself and appreciate the rural character of the Battlefield and the wider context.*"[88] That was so despite the permission being sought for a temporary period of 30 years, there being no direct effect on the Battlefield itself, and no discussion as to what level of contribution the appeal site, and the views that would be affected made to the overall significance of the Battlefield.

The Inspector also found the proposals would have a significant adverse effect on the character of the countryside[89], and that there was insufficient information on the potential archaeological impacts[90]. The proposals were found to conflict with the development plan as a whole,

---

87 APP/K2420/W/21/3266505

88 Ibid., at paragraph 26

89 Ibid., at paragraph 16

90 Ibid., at paragraphs 39-40

the NPPF, as well as EN-1 (which does not strictly apply), and so the appeal was dismissed.

The impact of the scheme on the historic environment was a key factor in the decision, which is perhaps unsurprising given the significance of the Bosworth Battlefield, not just as a registered heritage asset, but because of its national significance as the stage for a defining moment in history. In short, the Appellant had a high hurdle to jump, especially since it was accepted that there would be LTSH to the significance of the Battlefield, and the Inspector was not content with the information on potential archaeological impacts. That is reminder to promoters of solar (and any development) to ensure sufficient information is provided in support of proposals since it is difficult to determine the level of effect in the absence of all material facts, and a precautionary approach might dictate that the appeal is refused if the issue can't be dealt with by planning conditions or obligations.

The second appeal[91] concerned proposals for a 49.9MW solar farm and battery storage in Halloughton, Nottinghamshire. The appeal was heard at an inquiry and the decision issued allowing the appeal in February 2022. The main issues concerned the landscape and visual impacts of the scheme, the effect on heritage assets, and whether the proposals would conflict with the development plan. The decision letter records that changes were made to the scheme following the LPAs refusal and had been consulted on as part of the appeal process. The changes included the removal of panels close to the Halloughton Conservation Area, removal of panel close to a public footpath in the north of the site, and additional planting. The amendments were accepted because no party would be prejudiced by the appeal being determined on the basis of the amended scheme.[92]

The Inspector noted the positive context, both nationally and locally for the provision of renewable energy, as well as the inevitability that large

---

[91] APP/B3030/W/21/3279533

[92] Ibid., at paragraph 2

scale solar farms may result in landscape harm.[93] The site did not form part of a designated landscape and is not a "valued landscape" for the purposes of the NPPF, and so could not be regarded as highly sensitive. Further in respect of landscape and visual matters[94]:

(i) The Inspector acknowledged that the panels would "sit lightly on the affected fields with no material change to topography." This must be true of most if not all solar schemes.

(ii) Most of the site would be retained in agricultural use and used for sheep grazing. Again, this is common practice since the land can be used productively for agriculture, and the vegetation is maintained – it is a mutually beneficial way to manage the land.

(iii) Additional strategic planting was regarded as a major and significant beneficial effect.

(iv) While there would be a significant adverse effect on landscape character the nature of the site and the surrounds meant that it would be highly localised. The short-term construction effects were given only limited weight, since they could not be avoided and the Inspector noted that "*...you cannot make an omelette without breaking a few eggs*".

(v) The mitigation planting was consistent with the objectives of the development plan as well as the Newark and Sherwood Landscape Character Assessment Supplementary Planning Document and would leave an enhanced landscape.

In respect of the historic environment, harmful effects were alleged to the adjacent conservation area, and a number of listed buildings including a Grade II* listed Manor Farmhouse. The inspector found less than

[93] Ibid., at paragraphs 11 and 32

[94] Ibid., at paragraphs 11 to 32

substantial harm to both the conservation area and a number of listed buildings, although he considered that the harm fell at the lower end of the spectrum and was "clearly and decisively" outweighed by "the very significant benefits of the scheme."[95]

The Inspector found the contribution of the scheme to climate change objectives, meeting the energy needs of 12,000 homes annually, attracted significant weight[96]. So too did the "substantial" 73% biodiversity net gain.[97] The Inspector's pragmatic approach to the points taken by objectors on the loss of agricultural land was that only a small proportion of the site would be permanently lost from agricultural use, and it would, in any event continue to be used for agriculture through grazing sheep.[98] The scheme was found to accord with the objectives of the relevant development plan and national planning policy read as a whole, and the appeal was allowed.

The decision demonstrates the benefit of amending a scheme post decision to address the reasons for refusal and mitigate impacts on the natural and historic environment. The decision also demonstrates how a robust planting scheme can not only mitigate the landscape and visual impacts of a scheme but give rise to positive benefits. Applicants and appellants would be well advised to design schemes that bring above positive landscape character reinforcement and enhancements in line with local guidance which is often contained in landscape character assessments. It is also notable that unlike the Bosworth Battlefield decision which didn't touch upon biodiversity, the Halloughton scheme gave rise to a very substantial 73% net gain which attracted significant weight in the planning balance, and undoubtedly helped to outweigh the harm caused.

---

[95] Ibid., at paragraph 77

[96] Ibid., at paragraph 55

[97] Ibid., at paragraph 59

[98] Ibid., at paragraph 72

The final decision concerns an appeal which was determined following a hearing on 5 April 2022.[99] The parties were not legally represented, and two planning officers appeared on behalf of the Council. The main issues were the effect of the proposed development on best and most versatile agricultural land, the surrounding rural landscape character in combination with other schemes approved nearby, and the benefits of the proposal. The factual context for the appeal is slightly unusual in that another solar scheme occupying broadly the same area (35.67 ha) as the appeal site had been granted permission by the local authority prior to the hearing, which the inspector regarded as "a material consideration of significant weight."[100]

The Appellant's reports explained that 23.1 ha of the site to be developed would be on Grade 2 agricultural land, with the remaining area classified as moderate quality agricultural land (Grade 3b). By contrast the scheme approved by the Council avoided any Grade 2 land altogether, and BMV land occupied by the scheme was only 12.7 ha. Accordingly, the Inspector concluded that the scheme did not demonstrate that it would be necessary for all of the agricultural land within the appeal site to be used for the siting of the proposed array or that poorer quality land was being used in preference to higher quality land.[101] In short, it appears that the Appellant defeated its own case by securing planning permission on adjacent land containing lower quality agricultural land.

It is interesting that in dismissing the scheme the Inspector relied on the planning practice guidance discussed in chapter 3 above, as well as the 25 March 2015 WMS since both documents predate the Government's latest policy, statements, and commitments in respect of solar energy development, and arguably conflicts with the position proposed to be taken to nationally significant solar projects in respect of impacts on best and most versatile agricultural land.

[99] Land north of The Street, Cawston, Norfolk **APP/K2610/W/21/3278065**

[100] Ibid., at paragraph 4

[101] Ibid., at paragraphs 16-18.

As is to be expected, the Inspector attributed significant weight to the climate emergency,[102] and noted the significant environmental benefit of renewable energy and the economic benefits that would arise.[103] There was an unspecified level of Biodiversity Net Gain which was only given moderate weight in the planning balance because it was not secured beyond the lifetime of the scheme,[104] and was thus time limited. That is a conclusion which doesn't sit easily with the "greater significance" of the loss of BMV which was similarly time limited,[105] but which was sufficient alone to outweigh all the benefits of the scheme listed above in addition to the merits of site selection and social economic benefits which also achieved moderate weight in the planning balance.

There will be many more decisions in due course, including in respect of an appeal for a 49.9MW scheme near Cullompton in Mid Devon.[106] The appeal has been recovered by the Secretary of State and the decision is likely to be of significant interest to professional operating in the solar energy sector as well as LPAs and other stakeholders.

Given how few recent decisions there are, it is difficult at this stage to draw out consistent themes to guide future appeals. What does emerge is that the weight to be given to the contribution of renewable energy to combatting climate change is likely to be significant, but that is unsurprising given the background context and support for solar energy development explored throughout this book. What is also clear is that the national imperative to increase the deployment of solar technology won't always be enough, and there will be times when the harm outweighs the benefits. That is also to be expected. Applicants and appellant should ensure that they fully address the potential harms, look to maximise benefits, and incorporate effective mitigation to ensure that

---

[102] Ibid., at paragraph 28

[103] Ibid., at paragraphs 29 and 30

[104] Ibid., at paragraph 31

[105] Ibid., at paragraph 38

[106] APP/Y1138/W/22/3293104

the case is presented as effectively as possible, engaging professional experts and counsel at an early stage in the project.

CHAPTER SIX

APPLICATIONS UNDER THE PA 2008

The process

There are six stages to the development consent process which was introduced by the PA 2008 in order to streamline the decision-making process for major infrastructure projects. The aim of the process is to be fairer and faster for communities and applicants alike, but it is widely regarded by promoters of solar schemes as complex, expensive, and time consuming, which goes some way to explaining the proliferation of 49.9MW schemes coming forward through the TCPA 1990 route. In some respects, the complexities of the process inhibit the ability to provide the summary which follows below, but the DCO process is unavoidable for very large schemes, and the Planning Inspectorate has now examined more than 100 nationally significant infrastructure projects. Very large schemes may also require compulsory acquisition[107] and/or temporary possession of land, and accordingly, it is absolutely necessary for applicants to take legal advice and assemble its team of experts early on before embarking on the process. The process is paper-heavy, front loaded, and legally complex, thus a significant amount of guidance and advice notes are available for every stage of the process which explain the requirements of the various regulations.[108] They are

[107] see Sections 122 and 123 of the PA2008 that set out the requirements and conditions for compulsory acquisition.

[108] Including the Infrastructure Planning (Applications: Prescribed Forms and Procedures) Regulations 2009, the Infrastructure Planning (Changes to, and Revocation of, Development Consent Orders) Regulations 2011, the Infrastructure Planning (Compulsory Acquisition) Regulations 2010, the Infrastructure Planning (Environmental Impact Assessment) Regulations 2017, the Infrastructure Planning (Interested Parties and Miscellaneous

available on the Inspectorate's National Infrastructure Planning website.[109]

The six stages are as follows:

(i) Pre-application, where applicants have a statutory duty to notify the Secretary of State of the proposed application and consult on the proposed project. It is the applicant's responsibility to provide all of the information to support the application including an ES, shadow HRA, draft Development Consent Order. Applicants are advised to hold pre-application discussions with the Planning Inspectorate about how the information should be submitted and prepared.[110] The Inspectorate offers a free service at the pre-application stage which is designed to help applicants in planning and carrying out their pre-application duties.

(ii) Once submitted the Planning Inspectorate on behalf of the Secretary of State has 28 days to decide whether or not the application meets the standards required to be accepted for examination.

(iii) At the pre-examination stage the Examining Authority ("ExA"), a planning inspector, or panel of planning inspectors, is appointed, and members of the public can register to become an Interested Party by making a Relevant Representation ("RR"). A RR is made in writing and should summarise a person's views on the application. The ExA will hold a

---

Prescribed Provisions) Regulations 2015, and the Infrastructure Planning (Examination Procedure) Rules 2010

[109] https://infrastructure.planninginspectorate.gov.uk

[110] A suggested order for submitted information is set out at https://infrastructure.planninginspectorate.gov.uk/legislation-and-advice/advice-notes/advice-note-six-preparation-and-submission-of-application-documents/

Preliminary Meeting to discuss the process of the examination. All Interested Parties will be invited to attend, although the hearing is procedural in nature, and the merits of the scheme are not discussed. A preliminary Meeting is similar to a CMC prior to planning inquiries, and decisions are made on dates for the submission of Written Representations and the need for Issue Specific Hearings.

(iv) The ExA has six months to carry out the next stage which is the examination[111]. The examination timetable will be set out as soon as practicable after the Preliminary Meeting. The main method of examination is by Written Representations, but Issue Specific Hearings can be held if the ExA consider them to be necessary. If Interested Parties request an Open Floor Hearing then one must be held. Once the examination has begun, the relevant local authority or authorities will be notified and invited to submit a Local Impact Report on the likely effects of the NSIP on their local area. An important part of the examination process is the exchange of questions and answers between the ExA and the Applicant and Interested Parties.

(v) The Recommendation and Decision stage is where the ExA prepares a report in respect of the application for the relevant Secretary of State which includes a recommendation. The Secretary of State then has three months to arrive at a decision on whether to grant or refuse the DCO.

(vi) The final stage in the decision is the post decision stage of six weeks when the decision may be challenged in the high court. A recent example of such a challenge is *R (oao Save Stonehenge World Heritage Site Limited) v. Secretary of State for Transport* [2021] EWHC 2161 (Admin), in which a DCO for the

[111] See the Infrastructure Planning (Examination Procedure) Rules 2010 for details of the process

construction of a new 13km route for the A303 between Amesbury and Berwick Down was challenged and quashed on grounds relating to heritage impact and the assessment of alternatives.

Flexibility and other matters

Applicants will want to build flexibility into the DCO to accommodate changes that may be required post consent, for example, to respond to different or new regulatory regimes. 'Limits of Deviation' can be used within a DCO to allow flexibility for small-scale adjustment to the size and location of the project. The Inspectorate's 'Advice Note Nine: Rochdale Envelope' sets out the following at paragraph 1.2:

> *"The 'Rochdale Envelope' approach is employed where the nature of the Proposed Development means that some details of the whole project have not been confirmed (for instance the precise dimensions of structures) when the application is submitted, and flexibility is sought to address uncertainty. Such an approach has been used under other consenting regimes (the Town and Country Planning Act 1990 and the Electricity Act 1989) where an application has been made at a time when the details of a project have not been resolved."*

The Advice Note acknowledges that the need for flexibility is identified in a number of NPSs, but that flexibility should not be abused. Applicants should ensure that the approach taken is clearly explained, with consistent and clearly defined parameters that are assessed in the ES, and that the evidence in the support of the application remains consistent. Applicants should assess the worst-case scenario and provide sufficient information to identify the main or likely significant effects of the project.

Alternatives

Applicants will want to be mindful of emerging policy on 'Alternatives' set out in EN-1, which makes clear that while it is not a general requirement of the NPS to consider alternatives or establish that the proposal represents the "best option", there will be some circumstances in which it is necessary for an applicant to do so. Applicants will need to be alive to the issue as failure to consider alternatives when required to do so can lead to the quashing of a DCO.[112]

Common Ground

Applicants should endeavour to produce Statements of Common Ground with relevant bodies such as Historic England, Natural England, the Environment Agency etc., to assist with the examination process, and understand the position of relevant stakeholders in the process at the earliest possible opportunity. The onus is on applicants, and early engagement can ensure that potential issues are resolved prior to, or during the application.

Previous Decisions

As with TCPA 1990 appeals, there have been few decisions on nationally significant solar development, but there have been two recent decisions that applicants and interested parties will want to take into consideration.

The first is the Cleve Hill Solar Park DCO Decision of the 28 May 2020[113]. The proposal is for a solar farm with the option of additional storage facilities with a total capacity of around 350MW in Kent. The examination considered a range of matters including energy need,

[112] See for example *R (oao Save Stonehenge World Heritage Site Limited) v. Secretary of State for Transport* [2021] EWHC 2161 (Admin)

[113] The Cleve Hill Solar Park Order came into force on 19th June 2020

landscape and visual effects, impact on the historic environment, agricultural land, water environment (including flooding and coastal defence), and safety and security, particularly in respect of the proposed battery storage element.

The ExA found that there would be major and significant adverse landscape effect on an area designated in the development plan for its high landscape value. There would be significant and long-term adverse effects on two residential properties as well as on the use of the Saxon Shore Way, long-distance footpath. The adverse impacts which were noted as being reversible upon decommissioning were considered to have moderate weight in the overall balance.

The ExA also found that there would be adverse effects on the settings of a number of designated heritage assets, including the serious erosion of the rural character surrounding a listed church which was found to contribute to the asset's significance. Moderate weight was given to that harm in the balance.[114] Additional harm was found in respect of the loss of Grade 3b agricultural land, but that attracted only "very little weight" in the overall balance.[115]

Against the harms, the ExA found unequivocal support for the Proposed Development in the UK Solar PV Strategy,[116] and attributed substantial weight to the contribution that the Proposed Development will make towards the need for additional renewable energy generation, consistent with local and national policies on sustainable development.[117] Accordingly, the ExA recommended that the Secretary of State should make the DCO and the Secretary of State agreed.

---

[114] ExA Report at paragraph 8.1.64

[115] Ibid., at paragraph 8.2.33

[116] https://www.gov.uk/government/publications/uk-solar-pv-strategy-part-1-roadmap-to-a-brighter-future

[117] Ibid., at paragraphs 5.5.67 and 5.6.2

The ExA's treatment of the proposed battery storage system (at paragraph 8.7) is interesting and will be of significance to solar farm promoters and objectors as there is a growing trend for battery storage to be co-located with solar development. Battery Energy Storage Systems do not fall under the NSIP regime[118] but have a valuable role to play in balancing intermittent renewable energy development, whether from NSIPs or TCPA 1990 development[119].

There was significant objection to the Cleve Hill DCO because of the proposed lithium-ion technology and well publicised battery fires which have undoubtedly given all stakeholders in the process some cause for concern. Accordingly, the issue was considered at a special session in one of the Issue Specific Hearings with technical input from several parties. It is fair to note that there is something of a lacuna in the guidance and legislation concerning large scale battery storage while regulation catches up with technology. Nonetheless, there are significant benefits to co-locating battery storage and solar including:

i) enabling the integration of intermittent renewables into the electricity system by creating a more balanced grid.

ii) increasing efficiency since conventional generators can only supply power, whereas batteries can both store and discharge power depending on the balance of supply and demand.

iii) replacing carbon-heavy generators and reducing fossil fuel pollutants; and

iv) ensuring security of supply and reducing black-out exposure, due to batteries' fast response to supply/demand gaps.

---

[118] Section 122(2) of the PA2008

[119] See for example APP/Y1138/W/22/3293104, an appeal concerning a 49.9MW solar farm and battery storage facility

Further, the technology is supported as a national level. To highlight three of the most recent policy statements to this effect:

(i) The British Energy Security Strategy explains that the Government will encourage "*all forms of flexibility*" in the energy system and will develop policy to enable investment in "*sufficient large-scale, long-duration electricity storage*". It also sets out support for solar that is co-located with other functions, including storage, to maximise the efficiency of land use.[120]

(ii) Draft NPS EN-1 highlights that storage has "*a key role*" to play in achieving net zero, and that it is needed to reduce costs and increase the reliability of the electricity system by storing surplus in times of low demand and supplying electricity when demand is higher.[121]

(iii) The Net Zero Strategy also makes clear that as we rapidly decarbonise energy systems, we must also de-risk the delivery challenge and provide flexibility in order to integrate renewables and balance their intermittency. Doing so will involve pursuing innovative solutions, including new storage technologies

Ultimately, the ExA found that the risk associated with the technology could be managed through the submission of a Battery Safety Management Plan as a requirement in the DCO[122] and attributed that element of the scheme "significant additional positive weight."[123]The Secretary of State saw no reason to disagree with the conclusions,[124] and

[120]April 2022 CD D18

[121]September 2021 CD D3-B 3.3.24-3.3.25

[122]ExA Report at paragraphs 8.7.64-8.7.69

[123]Ibid., at paragraph 10.2.9 and 10.2.17.

[124]Decision Letter at paragraph 4.176

while it might now be thought that the issue is finally resolved, parties should be alive to the objection,[125] and provide technical evidence where appropriate.

The second decision is in respect of an application for a DCO for Little Crow Solar Park[126] dated 5 April 2022 which, in common with Cleve Hill, was a proposal for a solar farm (approx. 150MW) and battery storage of up to 90MW. Many of the same issues arose for consideration as in the Cleve Hill examination, including landscape and visual impacts, the effect on the historic environment and biodiversity. The ExA recommended that the Order should be made, and the Secretary of State agreed. However, there were points of difference between the ExA's Report and the Secretary of State's Decision Letter.

The ExA had concerns over the candidate panel design with an output of 420w and found that it was a missed opportunity to provide a scheme with a greater maximum output.[127] Accordingly, development incorporating the lower rated panel was considered to be an inefficient use of land, and was a factor that the ExA considered weighed significantly against the need for the proposed development.[128] The ExA's recommendation was that the DCO should specify a minimum power rating for the installed solar panels,[129] but the Secretary of State disagreed concluding at paragraph 4.35 of the Decision Letter that he had no information on which to conclude that the Applicant would do anything other than *"make best efforts to make the Development as efficient*

---

[125] Again, see appeal reference APP/Y1138/W/22/3293104 for solar development in Mid Devon where the primary issue was the battery storage facility rather than the solar farm itself.

[126] The Little Crow Solar Park Order 2022 and comes into force on 27th April 2022.

[127] ExA Report at paragraph 6.2.22, a 535w panel would be 25% more productive

[128] Ibid., at paragraphs 4.9.74-4.978

[129] Ibid., at paragraph 8.2.14

as possible in terms of land use... The Secretary of State anticipates it would in most cases be in an operator's commercial interest to do so."

The ExA also considered that the "small scale" of output from the project[130] meant that the proposal's contribution to meeting the need for electricity attracted no more than moderate positive weight in the balance, but the Secretary of State considered that it was "*appropriate to accord substantial positive weight to the project due to the contribution it will make towards the decarbonisation of the UK's energy production.*"[131] The ExA's conclusion is at odds with the Cleve Park decision and arguably §3.1 of EN-1 which sets out that *"The IPC should give substantial weight to the contribution which projects would make towards satisfying this need when considering applications for development consent under the Planning Act 2008."*

The two decisions summarised above are too small a sample upon which to base any firm conclusions, but there is an obviously fertile factual and policy context for the promotion of solar energy development and that is unlikely to change in the short or medium term. The obvious direction of travel expressed through the British Energy Security Strategy, the draft NPSs and other documents is unequivocal support for solar energy development as an important part of the future energy mix, and the Secretary of State's willingness to attribute "substantial positive weight" to large scale solar schemes is confirmation of that.

[130] Ibid., at paragraph 6.2.21, the daily output would be around 0.06% of electricity demand in the UK on an average day in 2020

[131] Decision Letter at paragraph 4.141

CHAPTER SEVEN

POST CONSENT ISSUES

Legal Challenge

Following a decision, the most pressing concern for those involved in the process will be the potential for legal challenge. The purpose of this chapter is not to set out in detail the principles of judicial review, which is a topic that occupies very many books, but rather to give an overview of the process and potential outcomes. The timescale for challenging planning decisions and DCOs is short, and a claim must be made within six weeks. Accordingly, decisions should be reviewed promptly by interested parties and their lawyers to understand whether there are any grounds for challenging the decision, and what the prospects of success might be. A challenge to the decision of a decision taker either by judicial review or statutory review is not a review of the merits, but a challenge to the lawfulness of the decision. Accordingly, a party will have to establish a legal error to succeed in the challenge and for the decision to be quashed.

In respect of DCOs, section 118 of the PA 2008 sets out that legal challenges to DCO decisions, either granting or refusing consent must be brought by a claim for judicial review before the end of the period of 6 weeks beginning with the day after any of the following:

(i) The day on which the DCO was published, or

(ii) If later, the day on which the statement of reasons for making the DCO was published, or

(iii) The day on which the statement of reasons for refusal was published.

Since the challenge proceeds by way of judicial review, Part 54 of the Civil Procedure Rules ("CPR") applies which sets out the rules relating to the process including time limits, the requirements for acknowledging the claim, the consequences of not acknowledging, and costs.

Claims for both judicial review and planning statutory review pursuant to section 288 of the TCPA 1990 have a permission stage where a decision is made as to whether the claim should proceed to a full substantive hearing on the papers . CPR Rule 54.11A applies where the court wishes to hear submissions on certain matters before determining whether permission for judicial review should be allowed to proceed, but more often than not permission is decided without a hearing. If permission is refused, the Claimant can request that the decision is reconsidered at a hearing which defendants and other interested parties can attend. Permission can be refused, allowed on all grounds or allowed on some and refused on others.

Decisions on called-in applications under section 77 of the TCPA 1990 and appeals under section 78 are challenged pursuant to section 288 of the TCPA 1990 by a person "aggrieved". Whether a person is aggrieved for the purpose of section will depend on matters such as the participation of that person in the decision-making process and their motives for challenge; *Walton v The Scottish Minister* [2013] P.T.S.R 51 at [83]-[88].

Practice Direction 54D of the CPR governs statutory challenges pursuant to section 288 and sets out the requirements particular to the Planning Court.

Challenges to decisions of LPAs to grant planning permission should be made by a claim for judicial review. The remedy for disappointed applicants following refusal of an application for planning permission is to appeal to the Planning Inspectorate pursuant to section 78 of the TCPA 1990.

Claimants who meet with the requirements of CPR 45.41-45.42 may be entitled to Aarhus costs protection which limits liability for costs if certain conditions are met. The purpose of the protection is to ensure that the litigation is not "prohibitively expensive" which ultimately encourages public participation in the planning system and the enhanced protection of the environment. There is provision within the rules for a reciprocal costs cap for Defendants, and Defendants can also challenge the application for costs protection in principle, or in relation to the amount of costs.

Where a decision is quashed, it is of no effect, and the matter is remitted to the decision taker for redetermination. This can give rise to procedural complexities in terms of the need to update the evidence for the appeal or examination, considering whether further hearings are necessary, or whether an inquiry should sit again. There is also the potential for compensation to be paid by the Planning Inspectorate where the Inspectorate was at fault for a quashed decision, for which see *D2M Solutions Ltd v Secretary of State for Communities and Local Government* [2017] EWHC 2409 (Admin).

Correction Orders

Section 119 and schedule 4 of the PA 2008 provides a mechanism by which the decision-takers can correct errors in decision documents relating to a DCO following an application made by any person in the relevant period which is six weeks after the day on which the DCO was published, or six weeks after the day on which the statement of reasons for making or refusing the order is published if that is later. The process is relatively common and uncontroversial.

Amending consents

There are several reasons why changes might be required to planning permissions or DCOs after they are granted. Unforeseen issues can arise once development has commenced, or technological advancements might require a slightly different form or configuration of development. To prevent applicants having to go through the process of securing a new consent all over again, there are different mechanisms for securing amendments to a development which are summarised below. In respect of amendments to development permitted pursuant to the TCPA 1990:

(i) An application for a non-material amendment can be made pursuant to section 96A of the TCPA 1990. There is no statutory definition of 'non-material', which is ultimately a matter of planning judgement. The LPA is not required to consult on the application but has the discretion to do so if appropriate. The time period for determination is 28 days, but a longer period of time can be agreed between the parties. There is no right of appeal from the LPAs decision.

(ii) Section 73 of the TCPA is appropriate for securing minor material amendments to a planning permission through varying the conditions. Importantly, permission granted following a section 73 application takes effect as a new independent permission, and so LPAs should take care to ensure that conditions and obligations necessary to make the development acceptable in planning terms are repeated in the new permission. Section 73 cannot be used to extend the time in which a permission can implemented, and a LPA can only consider the question of conditions, it cannot change the description of development.[132] Accordingly, if applicants wish to preserve flexibility in a permission, they may wish to provide a broad description of development in the first place supported

[132] *Finney v Welsh Ministers* [2020] EWCA Civ 1868

by more detailed plans[133] and conditions which define the scope of the development. A section 73 application is considered against the development plan and all material considerations, and there is a route of appeal to the Planning Inspectorate.

In respect of amendments to NSIPs consented pursuant to the PA 2008 these are significantly more complex.[134] As with the TCPA 1990 regime, applicants can seek to make non-material or material amendments to a DCO, and there is no statutory definition of the terms "material" or "non-material." Government guidance gives advice on when a change may be regarded material or not; for example, a material change would be one that requires an updated Environmental Statement to address new or material different effects.[135]

Both processes require consultation and engage the Infrastructure Planning (Changes to, and Revocation of, Development Consent Orders) Regulations 2011 (as amended). On receipt of an application for a material change application, the Secretary of State will consider whether to appoint an Examining Body to hold an examination or make the decision.

If an examination is held the procedure is very similar to a DCO examination, and the process set out at Chapter 6 above. However, the examination must be completed within 4 months beginning with the day after the last day of the preliminary meeting, and the Examining Body's Report submitted to the Secretary of State no later than two months

[133] Although avoid specifying candidate technology since these matters move on quickly and could well change by the time the application or an appeal is determined.

[134] Guidance can be found at https://assets.publishing.service.gov.uk/government/uploads/system/uploads/attachment_data/file/485064/Making_changes_guidance_to_Development_Consent_Orders.pdf

[135] Ibid.

thereafter. The Secretary of State must then decide whether to grant consent for the change and amend the DCO within two months of receipt. It is undoubtedly a time-consuming process.

Non-material changes are common throughout the planning system, and while material changes are very common in relation to planning permissions, such changes are extremely rare in respect of DCOs with the first ever material amendment to a DCO approved by the Secretary of State for Transport in July 2022 in relation to the Able Marine Energy Park.[136] The approval secures amendments to the layout of the quay and to a footpath diversion.

[136] https://infrastructure.planninginspectorate.gov.uk/projects/yorkshire-and-the-humber/able-marine-energy-park/

CHAPTER EIGHT

THE FUTURE FOR SOLAR DEVELOPMENT

The Government's support for solar energy development is unequivocal, and the need to significantly accelerate the deployment of renewable energy development is imperative. Solar development is well placed to assist in meeting that need; it can be deployed quickly, it is cost effective, and importantly, its effects are reversible upon decommissioning.

The reversibility of effects is a compelling argument in favour of solar energy development because any harm associated with solar panels will be removed after 30-40 years. The duration of solar farms is relatively short compared to the enduring nature of the rural landscape, and the lifespan of heritage assets that were in place long before solar development and will remain long after.

That being said, solar farms can be large developments – some are very large, and the effects of such development will sometimes be unacceptable. The delivery of solar farms on greenfield land will undoubtedly remain controversial for some, and that controversy may eventually prompt political intervention to impose restrictive conditions on solar development, although that seems unlikely at this stage. If it were to happen, such intervention would be extremely damaging to the solar industry and investor confidence as demonstrated through the Government's changed approach to onshore wind in 2013. The wind industry responded by going offshore; solar developers are also exploring the potential for floating solar development but the technology will take time to mature, and climate change targets won't wait. Nonetheless, the ability to screen solar farms in the landscape make them a less objectionable proposition to many objectors than turbines which can stand at over 200 metres and can be seen for miles.

There can be no doubt that renewable energy generation including solar energy has a fundamental role to play in the UK's energy strategy over the coming decade, both in terms of combatting the climate crisis and achieving net zero by 2050, and by providing energy security in an increasingly turbulent and unsettled global market.

Moreover, the direction of travel, expressed as recently as 7 April 2022 in the British Energy Security Strategy is overwhelmingly positive in favour of solar (while largely retaining the Government's position on onshore wind energy), and there will shortly be a consultation on amending planning rules to strengthen policy in favour of development on non-protected land, while ensuring communities continue to have a say and environmental protections remain in place. The designation of the draft NPSs which is likely to be in summer/ autumn 2022 will also further strengthen the support in favour of solar energy development for years to come both for nationally significant, and smaller developments.

MORE BOOKS BY LAW BRIEF PUBLISHING

'A Practical Guide to the EU Succession Regulation' by Richard Frimston
'A Practical Guide to Solicitor and Client Costs – 2nd Edition' by Robin Dunne
'Constructive Dismissal – Practice Pointers and Principles' by Benjimin Burgher
'A Practical Guide to Religion and Belief Discrimination Claims in the Workplace' by Kashif Ali
'A Practical Guide to the Law of Medical Treatment Decisions' by Ben Troke
'Fundamental Dishonesty and QOCS in Personal Injury Proceedings: Law and Practice' by Jake Rowley
'A Practical Guide to the Law in Relation to School Exclusions' by Charlotte Hadfield & Alice de Coverley
'A Practical Guide to Divorce for the Silver Separators' by Karin Walker
'The Right to be Forgotten – The Law and Practical Issues' by Melissa Stock
'A Practical Guide to Planning Law and Rights of Way in National Parks, the Broads and AONBs' by James Maurici QC, James Neill et al
'A Practical Guide to Election Law' by Tom Tabori
'A Practical Guide to the Law in Relation to Surrogacy' by Andrew Powell
'A Practical Guide to Claims Arising from Fatal Accidents – 2nd Edition' by James Patience
'A Practical Guide to the Ownership of Employee Inventions – From Entitlement to Compensation' by James Tumbridge & Ashley Roughton
'A Practical Guide to Asbestos Claims' by Jonathan Owen & Gareth McAloon
'A Practical Guide to Stamp Duty Land Tax in England and Northern Ireland' by Suzanne O'Hara
'A Practical Guide to the Law of Farming Partnerships' by Philip Whitcomb
'Covid-19, Homeworking and the Law – The Essential Guide to Employment and GDPR Issues' by Forbes Solicitors
'Covid-19 and Criminal Law – The Essential Guide' by Ramya Nagesh
'Covid-19 and Family Law in England and Wales – The Essential Guide' by Safda Mahmood
'A Practical Guide to the Law of Unlawful Eviction and Harassment – 2nd Edition' by Stephanie Lovegrove
'Covid-19, Brexit and the Law of Commercial Leases – The Essential Guide' by Mark Shelton
'A Practical Guide to Costs in Personal Injury Claims – 2nd Edition' by Matthew Hoe

'A Practical Guide to the General Data Protection Regulation (GDPR) – 2nd Edition' by Keith Markham
'Ellis on Credit Hire – Sixth Edition' by Aidan Ellis & Tim Kevan
'A Practical Guide to Working with Litigants in Person and McKenzie Friends in Family Cases' by Stuart Barlow
'Protecting Unregistered Brands: A Practical Guide to the Law of Passing Off' by Lorna Brazell
'A Practical Guide to Secondary Liability and Joint Enterprise Post-Jogee' by Joanne Cecil & James Mehigan
'A Practical Guide to the Pre-Action RTA Claims Protocol for Personal Injury Lawyers' by Antonia Ford
'A Practical Guide to Neighbour Disputes and the Law' by Alexander Walsh
'A Practical Guide to Forfeiture of Leases' by Mark Shelton
'A Practical Guide to Coercive Control for Legal Practitioners and Victims' by Rachel Horman
'A Practical Guide to Rights Over Airspace and Subsoil' by Daniel Gatty
'Tackling Disclosure in the Criminal Courts – A Practitioner's Guide' by Narita Bahra QC & Don Ramble
'A Practical Guide to the Law of Driverless Cars – Second Edition' by Alex Glassbrook, Emma Northey & Scarlett Milligan
'A Practical Guide to TOLATA Claims' by Greg Williams
'A Practical Guide to Elderly Law – 2nd Edition' by Justin Patten
'A Practical Guide to Responding to Housing Disrepair and Unfitness Claims' by Iain Wightwick
'A Practical Guide to the Construction and Rectification of Wills and Trust Instruments' by Edward Hewitt
'A Practical Guide to the Law of Bullying and Harassment in the Workplace' by Philip Hyland
'How to Be a Freelance Solicitor: A Practical Guide to the SRA-Regulated Freelance Solicitor Model' by Paul Bennett
'A Practical Guide to Prison Injury Claims' by Malcolm Johnson
'A Practical Guide to the Small Claims Track - 2nd Edition' by Dominic Bright
'A Practical Guide to Advising Clients at the Police Station' by Colin Stephen McKeown-Beaumont
'A Practical Guide to Antisocial Behaviour Injunctions' by Iain Wightwick

'Practical Mediation: A Guide for Mediators, Advocates, Advisers, Lawyers, and Students in Civil, Commercial, Business, Property, Workplace, and Employment Cases' by Jonathan Dingle with John Sephton
'The Mini-Pupillage Workbook' by David Boyle
'A Practical Guide to Crofting Law' by Brian Inkster
'A Practical Guide to Spousal Maintenance' by Liz Cowell
'A Practical Guide to the Law of Domain Names and Cybersquatting' by Andrew Clemson
'A Practical Guide to the Law of Gender Pay Gap Reporting' by Harini Iyengar
'A Practical Guide to the Rights of Grandparents in Children Proceedings' by Stuart Barlow
'NHS Whistleblowing and the Law' by Joseph England
'Employment Law and the Gig Economy' by Nigel Mackay & Annie Powell
'A Practical Guide to Noise Induced Hearing Loss (NIHL) Claims' by Andrew Mckie, Ian Skeate, Gareth McAloon
'An Introduction to Beauty Negligence Claims – A Practical Guide for the Personal Injury Practitioner' by Greg Almond
'Intercompany Agreements for Transfer Pricing Compliance' by Paul Sutton
'Zen and the Art of Mediation' by Martin Plowman
'A Practical Guide to the SRA Principles, Individual and Law Firm Codes of Conduct 2019 – What Every Law Firm Needs to Know' by Paul Bennett
'A Practical Guide to Adoption for Family Lawyers' by Graham Pegg
'A Practical Guide to Industrial Disease Claims' by Andrew Mckie & Ian Skeate
'A Practical Guide to Redundancy' by Philip Hyland
'A Practical Guide to Vicarious Liability' by Mariel Irvine
'A Practical Guide to Applications for Landlord's Consent and Variation of Leases' by Mark Shelton
'A Practical Guide to Relief from Sanctions Post-Mitchell and Denton' by Peter Causton
'A Practical Guide to Equity Release for Advisors' by Paul Sams
'A Practical Guide to Financial Services Claims' by Chris Hegarty
'The Law of Houses in Multiple Occupation: A Practical Guide to HMO Proceedings' by Julian Hunt
'Occupiers, Highways and Defective Premises Claims: A Practical Guide Post-Jackson – 2nd Edition' by Andrew Mckie

www.ingramcontent.com/pod-product-compliance
Ingram Content Group UK Ltd.
Pitfield, Milton Keynes, MK11 3LW, UK
UKHW020149290926
15471UKWH00004B/781

www.ingramcontent.com/pod-product-compliance
Ingram Content Group UK Ltd.
Pitfield, Milton Keynes, MK11 3LW, UK
UKHW051242300926
15471UKWH00016B/1727

9 781920 03